'LOVE IS THE SECRET INGREDIENT. ADD IT FREELY, AND WATCH THE MAGIC UNFOLD'

Teresa Cutter

FEEL GOOD BAKING

A healthier way to bake for you and your family

FEEL GOOD BAKING

A healthier way to bake for you and your family

TERESA CUTTER

SIMON & SCHUSTER

New York · Amsterdam/Antwerp · London · Toronto · Sydney · New Delhi

FEEL GOOD BAKING: A HEALTHIER WAY TO BAKE FOR YOU AND YOUR FAMILY
First published in Australia in 2025 by
Simon & Schuster (Australia) Pty Limited
Level 4, 32 York St, Sydney NSW 2000

10 9 8 7 6 5 4 3 2 1

New York Amsterdam/Antwerp London Toronto Sydney New Delhi
Visit our website at www.simonandschuster.com.au

© Teresa Cutter 2025

All rights reserved. No part of this publication may be reproduced, stored in a retrieval system, or transmitted in any form or by any means, electronic, mechanical, photocopying, recording or otherwise, without prior permission of the publisher.

ISBN: 9781761633294

Cover and internal design: Vanessa Russell, Raspberry Creative
Food photography: Paul Cutter ACS
Food styling: Teresa Cutter
Photo on page About Teresa: Steven Murray
Printed and bound in China by Asia Pacific Offset Limited

DEDICATION

This book is lovingly dedicated to Ciocia and Wujek, my dad—Stan the Man—my beautiful mum Maryla, my sister Carol, and my incredible husband Paul, who has stood beside me through it all.

To my amazing team at The Healthy Chef, to the readers, brands, and all the gorgeous souls who have supported me over the past twenty-five years, thank you from the bottom of my heart.

It's been a joyful, wild and rewarding journey creating The Healthy Chef and sharing the recipes that have nourished both body and soul.

Feel Good Baking is a celebration of good food and living a healthy, vibrant life. I hope it brings you as much joy in your kitchen as it has brought me in creating it.

With love,
Teresa x

CONTENTS

INTRODUCTION 9
BREAKFAST BAKES 11
WHOLESOME BREADS 37
CAKES + CUPCAKES 65
CHOCOLATE LOVE 105
PIES, TARTS + CRUMBLES 129
MUFFINS + SCONES 155
BISCUITS + COOKIES 179
SAVOURY BAKES 205
ESSENTIALS + BASICS 235
INGREDIENTS I LOVE TO USE 254
CONVERSIONS + MEASUREMENTS 260
INDEX 262
THANK YOU 269
ABOUT TERESA 271

INTRODUCTION

In a world where life moves at an ever-increasing pace, finding the time to cook and bake healthy foods can feel like a challenge. My latest creation, *Feel Good Baking*, is the perfect solution.

This is my ultimate collection of sweet and savoury bakes, drawn from my best-selling cookbooks *Purely Delicious*, *Healthy Baking*, *Earth to Table* and *Simple Healthy Recipes*. In this beautiful edition, I've brought together more than 100 uncomplicated, delicious recipes that will bring joy back into your kitchen and wellness into your life.

Crafted for the modern kitchen and the health-conscious cook, these recipes cater for all dietary preferences using wholefoods that make you feel good. Whether you're plant-based or gluten-free or just want to eat more pure, natural food that's good for you, there's something here for everyone. You'll also find top tips on ingredient swaps and suggestions on how to integrate these treats into a balanced lifestyle, making this book your go-to guide for guilt-free indulgence.

From everyday snacks to desserts that make special occasions even more memorable, *Feel Good Baking* is designed to be a kitchen staple for anyone who values health and flavour in equal measure. It's proof that healthy cooking doesn't have to be boring; it can indeed be purely delicious.

This is more than just a cookbook. It's a lifestyle companion, a tribute to the joy of baking, the power of nourishing food, and the art of eating well.

Enjoy,

Teresa Cutter

BREAKFAST BAKES

CINNAMON-DUSTED DOUGHNUTS

Take in the sweet aroma of these almond and cinnamon doughnuts as they're baking, then devour them with a cup of tea! Made with natural ingredients, they're a wholesome and satisfying alternative to their sugary store-bought counterparts.

LOW GI | WELLBEING | PALEO | GLUTEN-FREE

INGREDIENTS

150 g (1½ cups) almond meal

2 teaspoons gluten-free baking powder

½ teaspoon ground cinnamon

pinch of sea salt

2 free-range eggs

60 ml (¼ cup) olive oil

½ teaspoon vanilla extract

2 tablespoons maple syrup or honey

Cinnamon Dusting

2 tablespoons coconut sugar

1 teaspoon ground cinnamon

Makes 8 doughnuts

PREHEAT your oven to 160°C fan-forced.

GREASE 8 doughnut tins with butter or oil and set aside.

COMBINE almond meal, baking powder, cinnamon and sea salt in a large bowl.

ADD eggs, olive oil, vanilla and maple syrup.

MIX until well combined.

PIPE batter into the prepared doughnut tins.

BAKE for 15–18 minutes.

REMOVE from the oven and cool slightly.

COMBINE ingredients for Cinnamon Dusting in a small bowl. Sprinkle over doughnuts and enjoy.

NOTES AND INSPIRATION

Add a pinch of turmeric to the cinnamon dusting—it will look and taste amazing.

MAUI HEALTH CRUNCH BREAKFAST COOKIES

These awesome cookies are designed to enhance performance, fill you up and reduce fatigue. They are the ideal on-the-go breakfast or healthy snack to support an active body.

HIGH FIBRE | PROTEIN | LOW GI | DAIRY-FREE

INGREDIENTS

250 g (2½ cups) rolled oats or rolled quinoa

120 ml (½ cup) pure maple syrup

150 g (½ cup) natural smooth peanut butter or almond butter

½ teaspoon ground cinnamon, optional

1 teaspoon vanilla extract

2 free-range eggs

120 g fresh Medjool dates, pitted and chopped, or raisins

60 g (⅓ cup) pumpkin seeds, plus extra for sprinkling

Makes 8 large or 10 smaller cookies

PREHEAT oven to 160°C and line a baking tray with baking paper.

COMBINE oats and half the maple syrup (60 ml) in a bowl, then spread the mix out onto the prepared baking tray. Bake for 15–20 minutes until lightly toasted then cool completely.

MEANWHILE, combine the peanut butter, remaining maple syrup, cinnamon, vanilla and eggs in a large bowl.

ADD the toasted oats, dates and pumpkin seeds. Mix well until combined.

DIVIDE the mix into 8 large cookies or 10 smaller cookies using an ice-cream scoop or spoon. Sprinkle with extra seeds for decoration. Flatten slightly with your fingers.

BAKE for 20 minutes until golden.

ALLOW to cool then enjoy.

NOTES AND INSPIRATION

One large, mashed banana can replace the eggs in this recipe. Cookies will store in an airtight container for up to 1 week. These can also be baked in a square baking tin as a muesli slice.

BAKED BLUEBERRY OATMEAL

This recipe is like eating blueberry and apple pie for breakfast! It's full of fibre and goodness that supports a healthy digestive system, as well as warming spices to bring this nourishing meal to life.

ANTIOXIDANTS | HIGH FIBRE | LOW GI | GUT FRIENDLY

INGREDIENTS

100 g (1 cup) rolled oats

1 tablespoon golden flaxseed (linseed) meal

250 ml (1 cup) almond milk

¼ teaspoon sea salt

1 red apple, grated

½ teaspoon ground cinnamon

1 teaspoon vanilla extract

½ teaspoon baking powder

1 tablespoon maple syrup (optional), plus extra to serve

120 g (1 cup) blueberries, plus extra for garnish

2 tablespoons flaked almonds (optional)

Greek yoghurt or coconut yoghurt, to serve

Serves 2

COMBINE oats, flaxseed meal, milk and sea salt in a bowl.

COVER and place in the fridge overnight.

PREHEAT your oven to 170°C fan-forced.

REMOVE soaked oatmeal from the fridge and add grated apple, cinnamon, vanilla, baking powder and maple syrup, if desired.

FOLD through blueberries.

SPOON the mix into a suitable baking dish or 2 heatproof serving bowls.

GARNISH with a sprinkle of flaked almonds and scatter with a few extra blueberries.

BAKE for 25–30 minutes or until cooked through.

REMOVE from the oven and serve with a dollop of Greek yoghurt or coconut yoghurt with a drizzle of maple syrup.

NOTES AND INSPIRATION

Add one small, grated carrot and a pinch of nutmeg to make a delicious carrot cake oatmeal. Top with vanilla yoghurt and enjoy. Use quinoa flakes in place of oats for a gluten-free version.

QUINOA PANCAKES WITH ORANGE BLOSSOM HONEY

Here is a gluten-free and healthy recipe for pancakes made with quinoa that is also very yummy. These pancakes, drizzled with the seductive flavours of orange and vanilla, are perfect for a Sunday morning breakfast. It's important to use the whole quinoa seeds and not just the derived flour when making these pancakes as they produce the best results in both texture and taste.

PROTEIN | HIGH FIBRE | WELLBEING | GLUTEN-FREE

INGREDIENTS

200 g (1 cup) quinoa (whole raw grain)

1 tablespoon ground flaxseed (linseed)

325 ml (1⅓ cups) milk of any kind

1 teaspoon vanilla paste

¼ teaspoon ground cinnamon

2 free-range eggs

½ teaspoon bicarbonate of soda (baking soda)

2 bananas, mashed

macadamia nut oil, olive oil or clarified butter for cooking

Orange Blossom Honey

2 whole oranges

1 tablespoon honey

½ teaspoon vanilla paste

Serves 2

COMBINE quinoa, flaxseed and milk in a bowl and soak for at least 1 hour. For best results leave to soak overnight.

PLACE the soaked mixture in a high-performance blender along with vanilla, cinnamon, eggs and bicarbonate of soda.

BLEND until smooth and creamy.

REMOVE and fold in the mashed bananas by hand.

COOK spoonfuls of the pancake mix in a pan over low–medium heat until golden.

SERVE with orange blossom honey or pure maple syrup.

To make Orange Blossom Honey:

COMBINE the zest of 1 orange and the juice of 2 oranges in a pan with the honey and vanilla.

REDUCE the liquid until thickened then spoon over the pancakes.

NOTES AND INSPIRATION

Grated apple can be used in place of banana. Use maple syrup or rice malt syrup in place of honey.

BLUEBERRY AND BANANA PANCAKES

This is my delicious flourless pancake recipe packed full of wholefood goodness. Made from eggs, smashed banana, almonds and lush blueberries, these pancakes are the perfect healthy indulgence. They're also a great way to help your body refuel.

PROTEIN | HIGH FIBRE | GLUTEN-FREE | ANTIOXIDANTS

INGREDIENTS

2 ripe bananas (250 g), mashed

2 free-range eggs

100 g (1 cup) almond meal

1 tablespoon ground flaxseed (linseed)

½ teaspoon gluten-free baking powder

1 teaspoon ground cinnamon

125 g blueberries, optional

olive oil or macadamia nut oil, for cooking

natural yoghurt, to serve

Serves 2

COMBINE mashed banana and eggs.

ADD almond meal, flaxseed, baking powder and cinnamon. Fold in blueberries, if using.

REST for 5 minutes.

HEAT a pan over a low heat and add a little olive oil. For each pancake, spoon 2 tablespoons of pancake batter into the pan to form a circle and flatten slightly with the back of your spoon.

COOK over a very low heat. Take your time and don't rush. Flip over and finish cooking.

SERVE and enjoy your pancakes with natural yoghurt.

NOTES AND INSPIRATION

Use ricotta in place of the banana for yummy gluten-free ricotta hotcakes.

APPLE AND CINNAMON BREAD

Sweet red apples or Golden Delicious apples are the perfect ingredient to make this pure and amazing bread. This is a no fuss, one-bowl bread that can be easily whipped up in around 10 minutes. There's no need to add any sugar as the apple provides enough sweetness. Serve with your favourite cup of tea and a side of lemon.

HIGH FIBRE | WELLBEING | DAIRY-FREE

INGREDIENTS

- 500 g red apples, grated with the skin
- 60 ml (¼ cup) pure maple syrup
- 3 free-range eggs
- 120 ml (½ cup) olive oil
- 80 ml (⅓ cup) almond milk or kefir
- 3 teaspoons baking powder
- ½ teaspoon ground cinnamon
- 1 teaspoon vanilla paste or extract
- ¼ teaspoon sea salt
- 240 g (2 cups) wholemeal spelt flour
- 120 g (1¼ cups) walnuts, optional

Makes 1 loaf

PREHEAT your oven to 170°C fan-forced. Line a 26 x 10.5 cm loaf tin with baking paper at the base and sides.

COMBINE apple, maple syrup, eggs, oil, milk, baking powder, cinnamon, vanilla and salt in a bowl and mix well. I love using my hands for this, to make sure all the ingredients really get around the grated apple.

ADD the wholemeal spelt flour, followed by the walnuts and mix through lightly. It's important not to over-mix.

SPOON mixture into your loaf tin. At this point you can choose to bake as-is or garnish your bread with sliced apple and a little cinnamon or coconut sugar, which will create a lovely, caramelised flavour over the top of the apple.

BAKE for 50 minutes or until skewer inserted comes out clean.

REMOVE from the oven and allow to cool for 1 hour before turning bread out.

NOTES AND INSPIRATION

Fold through a handful of chopped raisins before baking. This bread will keep up to 5 days in the fridge. It's also delicious lightly toasted and devoured with a little butter.

APPLE AND MAPLE DUTCH BABY

A Dutch baby is like an embellished Yorkshire pudding, made with a crepe batter and baked in the oven to puff up in spectacular glory. Enjoy hot straight from the oven, drizzled with maple syrup and topped with a generous dollop of Greek yoghurt.

GUT-FRIENDLY | ENERGISING | HIGH FIBRE

INGREDIENTS

2 generous tablespoons of butter

2 large pink lady apples, peeled and thinly sliced

60 ml (¼ cup) pure maple syrup

3 large free-range eggs

125 ml (½ cup) milk of any kind

1 teaspoon vanilla extract

70 g (½ cup) spelt flour or gluten-free flour

pinch of sea salt

Embellishments

Icing sugar, maple syrup, Greek yoghurt, blueberries

Serves 2–3

PREHEAT your oven to 220°C fan-forced.

MELT the butter in a cast-iron pan over a medium heat and add the apples and maple syrup.

SAUTÉ until the apples are softened and wonderfully syrupy.

WHISK together the eggs, milk and vanilla in a bowl. Add the flour and salt and mix to form a smooth batter.

POUR the batter over the apples in the hot pan and place in the oven immediately.

BAKE for 15 minutes, until puffed and golden.

SERVE hot, straight from the oven with your choice of embellishments.

NOTES AND INSPIRATION

The more apples the better in this recipe.

BANANA, COFFEE AND WALNUT BREAD

This makes the perfect breakfast bread when you want something quick and easy to accompany your morning coffee. It's gluten-free and caressed with heart-healthy extra-virgin olive oil and a generous scattering of omega-3-rich walnuts for added crunch.

LOW CARB | PROTEIN | GUT FRIENDLY | GLUTEN-FREE

INGREDIENTS

500 g ripe banana, chopped

3 large free-range eggs

60 ml (¼ cup) milk, any kind

125 ml (½ cup) extra-virgin olive oil

2 teaspoons vanilla extract

90 g (½ cup) coconut sugar

2 tablespoons instant coffee powder

180 g (1¼ cups) brown rice flour

125 g (1¼ cups) almond meal

2 teaspoons baking powder

½ teaspoon bicarbonate of soda (baking soda)

180 g (1¾ cups) walnuts

Embellishments

Ricotta, tahini, carob molasses

Makes 1 loaf

PREHEAT your oven to 160°C fan forced. Grease and line a loaf tin with baking paper.

COMBINE bananas, eggs, milk, olive oil and vanilla in a food processor or blender and mix until smooth. Add the coconut sugar and coffee powder and mix again for a few seconds until combined.

POUR into a large mixing bowl and add the rice flour, almond meal, baking powder and baking soda. Mix well and fold in the walnuts at the very end.

SPOON into the prepared loaf tin. Decorate the top with a sliced banana if you have any left over.

BAKE for 50–60 minutes or until cooked through. Make sure to test the cake after 45 minutes as baking times sometimes vary based on your own oven.

REMOVE from the oven and cool for 1 hour in the tin, then transfer to a board to finish cooling.

SERVE on its own or lavishly topped with ricotta, tahini and a drizzle of carob molasses.

NOTES AND INSPIRATION

Serve with your choice of espresso or latte.

GLUTEN-FREE BANANA BREAD

You'll find this version to be a nice change from store-bought and cafe-style banana breads that are typically high in refined white flour, sugar and saturated fats. I love using macadamia nut oil when baking. It's a delicious source of monounsaturated fats that help support good health.

HIGH FIBRE | GRAIN-FREE | DAIRY-FREE | GLUTEN-FREE

INGREDIENTS

- 300 g (about 3) ripe bananas, mashed, plus 1 extra to decorate (optional)
- 3 free-range eggs
- 60 ml (¼ cup) honey or pure maple syrup
- 60 ml (¼ cup) olive or macadamia nut oil
- 1 teaspoon vanilla extract
- ½ teaspoon ground cinnamon
- 2 teaspoons gluten-free baking powder
- 200 g (2 cups) almond meal
- 1 tablespoon ground flaxseed (linseed)

Makes 1 loaf

PREHEAT your oven to 160°C fan-forced. Line a 26 x 10.5 cm loaf tin with baking paper.

COMBINE mashed banana, eggs, honey, oil, vanilla, cinnamon and baking powder in a large bowl.

ADD the almond meal and flaxseed and mix well.

SPOON the banana bread mixture into the tin. At this stage you can garnish the top with a halved banana before baking if you like.

BAKE for 45–50 minutes (a skewer inserted into the centre should come out dry when cooked through).

REMOVE from the oven and allow to cool before turning out the loaf. Keep in the fridge, covered, for up to 1 week.

NOTES AND INSPIRATION

Serve with ricotta and honey, or simply toasted and enjoy with a cup of lemon tea. I like to decorate the top of my banana bread before baking with sliced banana or a handful of chopped walnuts and a light sprinkle of cinnamon.

BLUEBERRY MUFFINS

One of these high-protein blueberry muffins is practically a meal in itself and is ideal for breakfast on the run served with a cup of your favourite tea. This muffin packs quite a punch—it's high in protein, B vitamins and antioxidants, which will help fill you up, keep blood sugars stable and keep you energised all day long.

GRAIN-FREE | PROTEIN | LOW GI | GLUTEN-FREE

INGREDIENTS

300 g (3 cups) almond meal

2 teaspoons gluten-free baking powder

4 free-range eggs

60 ml (¼ cup) olive oil

1 teaspoon ground cinnamon

80 ml (⅓ cup) honey or pure maple syrup

1 red apple, skin on, chopped into small chunks or coarsely grated

200 g blueberries (fresh or frozen)

Makes 10 muffins

PREHEAT the oven to 170°C fan-forced. Line a muffin tin with paper cases.

COMBINE almond meal and baking powder in a large mixing bowl.

ADD the eggs, oil, cinnamon and honey to form a batter.

FOLD in the apple and blueberries.

DIVIDE the batter between each muffin case.

BAKE for 35–40 minutes until cooked through and golden.

NOTES AND INSPIRATION

Hazelnut meal also works really well for this recipe and marries perfectly with the apple and blueberry.

FRENCH TOAST PUDDING WITH BANANA AND BLUEBERRY

Perfect for a warming weekend breakfast, this pudding is satisfying to the core. It's a great way to use up any leftover stale bread and it can be enjoyed hot or cold. The whole family will love it!

WELLBEING | ENERGISING | ALL NATURAL

INGREDIENTS

350 g leftover bread (your choice: challah, brioche, gluten-free, fruit bread)

5 large free-range eggs

625 ml (2½ cups) milk of any kind

2 teaspoons vanilla extract

2 tablespoons raw honey

pinch of nutmeg

2 lady finger bananas, halved

125 g blueberries

Serves 6–8

PREHEAT your oven to 160°C fan-forced.

SLICE the bread and place in a baking dish.

COMBINE eggs, milk, vanilla, honey and nutmeg in a bowl and whisk well.

POUR the egg mixture over the bread and allow to sit for 15 minutes, which allows the bread to soak up the milk.

ARRANGE the banana on top and sprinkle over the blueberries.

BAKE for 45–50 minutes until the egg has set. If necessary, cover with foil halfway during cooking to prevent over-browning.

REMOVE from the oven and serve at the table. Delicious hot or cold.

NOTES AND INSPIRATION

Add other fruits such as fresh figs or blackberries.

FRUIT AND RYE LOAF

This wholesome fruit loaf is high in fibre, prebiotics and probiotics that support digestive health. Naturally sweetened with honey and raisins, it's delicious toasted and spread with butter or cream cheese.

WELLBEING | HIGH FIBRE | GUT FRIENDLY

INGREDIENTS

240 g (2 cups) rye flour

200 g (1⅓ cups) raisins (see Notes)

1 teaspoon sea salt flakes

1 teaspoon baking powder

½ teaspoon bicarbonate of soda (baking soda)

250 ml (1 cup) natural kefir or yoghurt

60 ml (¼ cup) honey

60 ml (¼ cup) water

Makes 1 loaf

PREHEAT your oven to 160°C fan-forced. Grease a loaf pan with olive oil and dust with rye flour.

COMBINE rye flour, raisins, salt, baking powder and bicarbonate of soda in a large bowl.

POUR in the kefir, honey and water, then mix to make a thick, wet dough.

SPOON the dough into the prepared pan and level it out with the back of a spoon. Cover with a layer of baking paper, then seal with foil.

BAKE for 60–70 minutes, then remove the foil and test the loaf to see if it's cooked through. Cool completely.

SERVE the loaf when it's fully cold. Perfect with a cup of tea or long black. It's delicious lightly toasted the next day for breakfast.

NOTES AND INSPIRATION

This loaf is also delicious made without the dried fruit. It can be served with sweet and savoury toppings. Try it with avocado and salt or cream cheese or ricotta. Store in the fridge for up to 1 week.

WHOLESOME BREADS

PALEO PUMPKIN BREAD

This scrumptious loaf is made from grated fresh pumpkin, free-range eggs and almonds. A great source of antioxidants and protein, this is the perfect 'bread of champions' to nourish and energise your body.

HIGH FIBRE | GRAIN-FREE | DAIRY-FREE | GLUTEN-FREE

INGREDIENTS

450 g raw pumpkin, grated

4 free-range eggs

½ teaspoon sea salt

pinch of nutmeg

60 ml (¼ cup) olive oil

300 g (3 cups) almond meal

2 teaspoons gluten-free baking powder

handful of pumpkin seeds, to sprinkle

Makes 1 loaf

PREHEAT your oven to 160°C fan-forced. Line a 26 x 10.5 cm loaf tin with baking paper at the base and sides.

COMBINE pumpkin, eggs, salt, nutmeg and oil in a bowl.

ADD the almond meal and baking powder and mix well.

SPOON the mixture into the loaf tin and sprinkle the top with pumpkin seeds.

BAKE for approximately 1½ hours or until firm to touch.

REMOVE from the oven and allow to rest for 1 hour before removing from the tin.

COOL and enjoy.

NOTES AND INSPIRATION

Try topped with macadamia nut butter and a little honey.

POTATO BUNS

This recipe, created by my great aunt Ciocia, is based on a Polish bread roll. These buns are soft, fluffy and perfect topped with good butter and devoured with a warming bowl of soup.

WHOLEFOOD | WELLBEING | STRESS RELIEF

INGREDIENTS

400 g potato, peeled and cut into chunks

250 g (2 cups) spelt flour

1 teaspoon sea salt

3 teaspoons baking powder

100 g butter, room temperature

125 ml (½ cup) warm milk

Makes 12 buns

BOIL potatoes until tender, then drain.

MASH the potatoes or put through a potato ricer, then cool. Set aside 250 g mashed potato to make these buns.

PREHEAT your oven to 200°C fan-forced. Line a baking tray with baking paper.

COMBINE spelt flour, salt and baking powder. Rub in the butter until mixed through.

ADD the 250 g mashed potato, followed by the warm milk, and lightly mix to make a soft dough. Turn out the dough onto a floured surface and cut into rounds. Alternatively, you can cut into wedges using a sharp knife. Place them on the baking tray.

BAKE for 20 minutes until golden. Cool slightly before serving.

NOTES AND INSPIRATION

Simply top with butter or enjoy with good jam and a dollop of yoghurt.

BANANA AND CHIA BREAD WITH ESPRESSO CARAMEL

My gorgeous vegan banana bread is filled with the goodness of oats and omega-3-rich chia seeds. I've frosted mine with coconut yoghurt but it's equally delicious with a dollop of Greek yoghurt or just served on its own with an almond milk latte.

VEGAN | DAIRY-FREE | HIGH FIBRE | WHOLEFOOD

INGREDIENTS

2 tablespoons chia seeds

125 ml (½ cup) water

125 ml (½ cup) extra-virgin olive oil

60 ml (¼ cup) pure maple syrup

2 teaspoons vanilla extract

300 g ripe lady finger bananas, mashed

90 g (⅔ cup) rice flour

125 g (1 cup) oat flour or gluten-free flour

3 teaspoons gluten-free baking powder

coconut yoghurt, to serve (optional)

Espresso Caramel (p 44), to serve

Serves 12

PREHEAT your oven to 160°C fan-forced. Line a 26 x 10.5 cm loaf tin with baking paper.

COMBINE chia seeds and water and set aside for 15 minutes to make a chia gel.

PLACE chia gel in a large bowl with the olive oil, maple syrup, vanilla and banana and mix.

ADD rice flour, oat flour and baking powder and combine.

SPOON the mixture into the tin.

BAKE for 45–60 minutes or until cooked through and firm to touch.

REMOVE from the oven and cool completely.

SERVE on its own or lavishly topped with coconut yoghurt and Espresso Caramel.

NOTES AND INSPIRATION

Add a handful of walnuts before baking or when serving.

ESPRESSO CARAMEL

My natural and wholefood version of a creamy caramel sauce that's free from refined sugars. This caramel sauce is perfect to serve over banana bread or even drizzled over a fresh ripe banana split.

GLUTEN-FREE | PLANT-BASED | DAIRY-FREE | PURELY DELICIOUS

INGREDIENTS

10 fresh dates, pitted

250 ml (1 cup) filter coffee

125 ml (½ cup) coconut milk

Makes 375 ml (1½ cups)

COMBINE dates and coffee in a blender.

BLEND for a few minutes until smooth and creamy.

ADD coconut milk and blend for a few more seconds until mixed through the dates and coffee emulsion.

SERVE over banana bread.

NOTES AND INSPIRATION

To turn this into the yummiest chocolate sauce, replace filter coffee with hot water and add vanilla extract, a pinch of sea salt, 3 tablespoons cacao powder and a little extra water.

BUTTERMILK LOAF

This recipe is based on a classic Irish soda bread but uses much more liquid to make the dough. You could also use kefir or natural yoghurt in place of buttermilk; the results will be the same. It's kind to the tummy and absolutely delicious to eat.

PROTEIN | HEART HEALTHY | ALL NATURAL

INGREDIENTS

2 tablespoons raw honey or pure maple syrup

1 large free-range egg

500 ml (2 cups) buttermilk

60 ml (¼ cup) extra-virgin olive oil

380 g (3¼ cups) spelt flour or gluten-free flour

½ teaspoon baking powder

2 teaspoons bicarbonate of soda (baking soda)

½ teaspoon salt

3 tablespoons seeds (I used sesame, poppy and hemp)

Makes 1 loaf

PREHEAT your oven to 180°C fan-forced. Line a 26 x 10.5 cm loaf tin with baking paper.

COMBINE honey, egg, buttermilk and olive oil in a mixing bowl.

COMBINE spelt flour, baking powder, bicarbonate of soda and salt in another bowl.

SIFT the dry ingredients so that the baking powder and bicarb mix evenly through the flour.

POUR the buttermilk mixture into the flour and gently fold through until combined. Don't over mix.

SPOON the bread mixture into the prepared tin and smooth the top.

SCATTER generously with seeds.

BAKE for 45–50 minutes until cooked through.

REMOVE from the oven and cool in the tin for 10 minutes before removing to cool completely on a rack or board.

ENJOY at room temperature with anything you desire.

NOTES AND INSPIRATION

This bread is perfect smeared with good-quality butter or ricotta and whole fruit jam. Or try it lightly toasted and topped with smashed avocado and salt, then enjoy with a hearty bowl of pumpkin soup.

SEEDY GLUTEN-FREE BREAD

This loaf is delicious toasted in a non-stick pan, then spread with a dollop of ricotta and a little honey. Every slice is full of healthy fats, protein and fibre to support healthy digestion, lean, toned muscle and overall wellbeing.

GLUTEN-FREE | HEART HEALTHY | LOW CARB

INGREDIENTS

30 g (¼ cup) ground golden flaxseeds

30 g (¼ cup) hemp seeds

30 g (¼ cup) sunflower seeds

30 g (¼ cup) sesame seeds

30 g (¼ cup) poppy seeds

2 tablespoons nigella seeds

125 ml (½ cup) water

5 free-range eggs

60 ml (¼ cup) olive oil

150 g (1½ cups) almond meal

40 g (¼ cup) tapioca flour

1 teaspoon sea salt

2 teaspoons gluten-free baking powder

Makes 1 loaf

PREHEAT your oven to 160°C fan-forced and line a loaf tin with baking paper.

COMBINE all the seeds and water in a bowl.

ALLOW to stand for 15 minutes and thicken slightly.

BEAT the eggs until creamy and light.

POUR in the olive oil, then add the almond meal, tapioca flour, salt, baking powder and seed mixture.

SPOON the batter into the prepared loaf tin.

BAKE for 45–50 minutes until cooked through.

REMOVE and cool completely.

NOTES AND INSPIRATION

Store in the fridge for up to 1 week. Slice and freeze if desired.

THE PERFECT FOCACCIA

This genius focaccia is wonderfully soft and delicious to eat with generous amounts of heart-healthy olive oil. Feel free to add your choice of toppings before and after you bake it. It works beautifully with a drizzle of salsa verde, pan-roasted zucchini and dollops of ricotta.

WELLBEING | STRESS RELIEF | ALL NATURAL

INGREDIENTS

500 g spelt flour

7 g (1 sachet or 2 teaspoons) dry yeast

10 g (2 teaspoons) baking powder

1 teaspoon sea salt

400 ml (1½ cups) room temperature/tepid water

3 tablespoons extra-virgin olive oil

2 tablespoons raw honey

Toppings

Rosemary, garlic, olive oil, pesto, ricotta, cherry tomatoes, oregano and flaked sea salt

Serves 12

COMBINE spelt flour, yeast, baking powder and salt in a mixing bowl.

POUR in the water, olive oil and honey and mix until combined and you have a soft, sticky dough. Mix well for 10 minutes using a stand mixer, until the dough gets more elastic. You'll see it come together at the end.

COVER the dough with cling film and leave to prove overnight in the fridge.

NEXT day, remove the dough from the fridge. Tip the dough from the bowl and place straight into a deep baking tray lined with baking paper and drizzled with generous amounts of olive oil. The size of the pan I used was 30 x 23 cm.

USING your hands, press down the dough to fit it into the tray and prove for 40 minutes. Top with your choice of toppings. I love pesto, ricotta and cherry tomatoes or simply scatter with smashed rosemary or oregano, flaked sea salt and olive oil.

PREHEAT your oven to 200°C fan-forced.

BAKE for 20–25 minutes until golden and cooked through. Remove from the oven.

COOL for at least 15 minutes before devouring.

NOTES AND INSPIRATION

This recipe works amazingly well with 100 per cent hydration (equal parts flour to water).

GLUTEN-FREE FOCACCIA

Make sure to use a good-quality gluten-free flour to make this recipe. I've made this bread using Caputo Gluten Free Flour as well as Bob's Red Mill, and both have turned out perfectly. Top with olive oil and oregano or scatter with halved cherry tomatoes before baking.

GLUTEN-FREE | ENERGISING | ALL NATURAL

INGREDIENTS

500 g gluten-free flour

7 g (1 sachet or 2 teaspoons) dry yeast

10 g (2 teaspoons) gluten-free baking powder

1 teaspoon sea salt

500 ml (2 cups) warm water

⅓ cup extra-virgin olive oil, plus extra to drizzle

2 tablespoons raw honey

1 teaspoon dried oregano

Serves 12

COMBINE flour, yeast, baking powder and salt in a bowl.

POUR in the water, olive oil and honey and mix well to form a sticky dough.

LINE a large baking tray with baking paper.

USING your hands, spread the dough over the tray to a depth of about 3 cm thickness.

COVER the dough with cling film and allow to prove for 1–2 hours until doubled in size.

USING your fingers, create dimples in the dough then drizzle with a little olive oil and sprinkle with dried oregano. The dough will deflate slightly, so allow it to sit uncovered for another 30 minutes.

PREHEAT your oven to 200°C fan-forced.

BAKE for 30 minutes or until cooked through and golden.

COOL completely before devouring.

NOTES AND INSPIRATION

Serve as a side to soups, or toast the next day and serve with ricotta, salsa verde or pesto. Try topping the focaccia with black grapes, rosemary and sea salt or cherry tomatoes, basil and pitted kalamata olives before baking.

SPELT AND KEFIR SODA BREAD

There's nothing like tearing into a crusty soda bread fresh from the oven. My recipe is easy to make and has a subtle sweetness and density that goes with just about anything sweet or savoury.

WELLBEING | WHOLEFOOD | HIGH FIBRE | GUT FRIENDLY

INGREDIENTS

120 g (1 cup) wholemeal spelt flour

120 g (1 cup) white spelt flour

1 tablespoon ground golden flaxseeds

1 teaspoon sea salt

1 teaspoon bicarbonate of soda (baking soda)

310 ml (1¼ cups) natural kefir

2 tablespoons extra-virgin olive oil

1 tablespoon honey

30 g (¼ cup) seeds of your choice (sesame, sunflower, etc), optional

Makes 1 loaf

PREHEAT your oven to 200°C fan-forced. Line a baking tray with baking paper.

COMBINE spelt flours, ground flaxseed, salt and bicarbonate of soda in a bowl and mix well.

COMBINE kefir, olive oil and honey in a separate bowl.

POUR the wet mixture over the dry ingredients and mix through lightly with a spoon. The dough should be lovely, sticky and moist, much like scone dough.

TIP the dough onto a floured surface and form into a round loaf, then transfer to the prepared baking tray. Flatten slightly. Brush the top of the dough with a little water or kefir and sprinkle with the seeds if using.

BAKE for 25 minutes until cooked through.

COOL for at least 30 minutes and enjoy.

NOTES AND INSPIRATION

Don't knead the dough too much, but just lightly enough for it to combine. This bread is delicious topped with avocado and a little sea salt, or butter and jam, or ricotta and honey.

HONEY AND RICOTTA BREAD

This is a spectacular bread that falls between a crusty loaf and a brioche, making it pleasurable to eat. I love to serve it with ricotta and a generous drizzle of honey.

ALL NATURAL | STRESS-RELIEF | ENERGISING

INGREDIENTS

500 g spelt flour, plus extra for kneading

1 teaspoon dry yeast

2 teaspoons baking powder

1 teaspoon sea salt

250 ml (1 cup) room temperature water

60 ml (¼ cup) extra-virgin olive oil

60 ml (¼ cup) raw honey

250 g firm ricotta, deli-style

rice flour or spelt flour, for dusting

Makes 1 loaf

COMBINE spelt flour, yeast, baking powder and salt in a mixing bowl.

ADD the water, olive oil, honey and ricotta.

MIX for 10 minutes using a stand mixer with the paddle attachment until the dough becomes elastic and comes together.

COVER the dough with cling film and leave overnight in the fridge to prove. This helps develop flavour and structure.

THE NEXT DAY, remove the dough from the fridge, dust with a little flour and form into a round loaf. Place on a piece of baking paper, dust generously with rice flour, then cover with a tea towel to stand for 45 minutes.

MEANWHILE, preheat your oven to 200°C fan-forced. Place a large cast-iron pot with a fitted lid in the oven to heat up.

TRANSFER the dough into the heated pot and cover with the lid.

BAKE for 30 minutes with the lid on, then remove the lid and continue baking the loaf for another 10 minutes until cooked through. The bread will brown quickly because of the added honey, but it's important to bake the loaf thoroughly. Cover with foil if needed.

COOL for 1 hour before devouring.

NOTES AND INSPIRATION

Any leftovers can be cut into chunks, toasted and used for a panzanella with juicy tomato, basil and aged balsamic vinegar.

KETO PILLOW BREAD

A keto favourite that's low in carbs and so wonderfully soft and delicious to eat. You can serve these breads topped with cream cheese, smashed avocado or a slice of buffalo mozzarella with tomato and fresh basil.

GLUTEN-FREE | PROTEIN | LOW CARB | ENERGISING | GUT FRIENDLY

INGREDIENTS

3 free-range eggs, separated

pinch of sea salt

60 g cream cheese, quark or labneh

Makes 8 breads

PREHEAT your oven to 160°C fan-forced. Line a baking tray with baking paper.

WHIP egg whites and salt into stiff peaks.

MIX cream cheese and egg yolks until smooth.

FOLD the egg whites into the egg yolk mixture.

DIVIDE the batter evenly into rounds on the baking tray.

BAKE for 20 minutes until golden.

COOL then enjoy.

NOTES AND INSPIRATION

Top with cream cheese, thyme and lemon-scented olive oil. Use as a delicious base for pizza.

SEEDED RYE, OAT AND SUNFLOWER BREAD

Rye flour is rich in minerals such as magnesium, zinc and iron as well as protein, B vitamins and fibre. I adore baking with rye as it's kind to my digestive system and helps stabilise my blood sugars.

PLANT-BASED | HIGH FIBRE | LOW GI | GUT FRIENDLY

INGREDIENTS

500 ml (2 cups) natural yoghurt

60 ml (¼ cup) molasses

60 ml (¼ cup) extra-virgin olive or avocado oil

140 g (1¼ cups) rye flour

125 g (1 cup) wholemeal spelt or kamut flour

60 g (½ cup) rolled oats

2 tablespoons ground flaxseeds

90 g (¾ cup) sunflower seeds, plus extra to garnish

3 teaspoons baking powder

Serves 12

PREHEAT your oven to 160°C fan-forced. Line a 26 x 10.5 cm loaf tin with baking paper.

COMBINE yoghurt, molasses and olive oil in a mixing bowl.

ADD rye flour, spelt flour, oats, flaxseeds, sunflower seeds and baking powder and mix lightly to form a dough.

SPOON into the loaf tin and sprinkle with sunflower seeds.

BAKE for 45–60 minutes until cooked through.

REMOVE from the oven and cool.

SERVE with your choice of yummy toppings.

NOTES AND INSPIRATION

Serve with sliced cheddar and seeded mustard or piccalilli, smoked salmon, cucumber and yoghurt dressing, or smashed mustardy eggs.

SWEETCORN BREAD

Filled with juicy corn kernels, this cornbread is easy to make, plus it's gluten-free and high in fibre and protein. It's perfect served with a side of black beans or smashed avocado and a dollop of yoghurt.

GUT FRIENDLY | ENERGISING | HIGH FIBRE | GLUTEN-FREE

INGREDIENTS

500 g sweet corn kernels

3 large free-range eggs

80 ml (⅓ cup) extra-virgin olive oil

250 ml (1 cup) natural yoghurt or kefir

pinch of sea salt

1 tablespoon raw honey

200 g (1¼ cups) quick-cook polenta, plus extra for dusting

1 teaspoon gluten-free baking powder

3 spring onions, finely sliced

90 g cheddar, grated

Serves 12

PREHEAT your oven to 180°C fan-forced. Lightly butter a 22 cm cast-iron pan and dust with polenta.

COMBINE corn, eggs, olive oil, yoghurt, salt, honey, polenta and baking powder in a food processor.

PROCESS until ingredients are mixed through and combined, then spoon the batter into a large bowl.

FOLD IN the spring onions and cheese.

SPOON the batter into the cast-iron pan.

BAKE for 45 minutes until cooked through and golden.

SERVE warm or at room temperature.

NOTES AND INSPIRATION

Fold through finely diced red capsicum or baby spinach leaves before baking. Serve alongside black beans, fresh limes, Greek yoghurt and smashed avocado. Make into individual muffins and top with feta or ricotta before baking.

CAKES + CUPCAKES

ORANGE AND OLIVE OIL TEA CAKE

A gorgeous all-time favourite at Healthy Chef HQ. We make this cake about once a week for entertaining, high tea and cooking events. Enriched with generous amounts of olive oil, this cake will become your favourite.

LOW GI | HEART HEALTHY | HIGH FIBRE | WHOLEFOOD

INGREDIENTS

2 free-range eggs

125 ml (½ cup) extra-virgin olive oil

125 ml (½ cup) raw honey

180 ml (¾ cup) milk of any kind

1 teaspoon vanilla extract

zest of 1 orange

180 g (1½ cups) wholemeal spelt flour

3 teaspoons baking powder

Caramelised Oranges (p 76), to serve (optional)

Serves 12

PREHEAT your oven to 160°C fan-forced. Line a 26 x 10.5 cm loaf tin with baking paper.

COMBINE eggs, olive oil, honey, milk, vanilla and orange zest in a mixing bowl.

ADD flour and baking powder and mix with a whisk until combined.

POUR into the prepared loaf tin.

BAKE for 45–60 minutes until cooked through.

COOL in the tin for 30 minutes then turn out to cool on a board or cake rack.

DECORATE with Caramelised Oranges if desired.

SERVE for morning or afternoon tea and enjoy.

NOTES AND INSPIRATION

For a gluten-free version, reduce milk to 125 ml (½ cup) and replace spelt flour with 155 g (1½ cups) almond meal combined with 100 g (⅔ cup) rice flour. This cake is also lovely iced or simply served plain.

SEMOLINA AND OLIVE OIL SYRUP CAKE

This is a Healthy Chef favourite that is super-moist and delicious; it's best served cold, straight from the fridge, embellished simply with a dollop of Greek yoghurt, which makes it perfect for dinner parties. Use a light-flavoured olive oil to make this cake.

HEART HEALTHY | ALL NATURAL | WELLBEING

INGREDIENTS

4 large free-range eggs

250 ml (1 cup) extra-virgin olive oil

90 g (½ cup) raw sugar

2 teaspoons vanilla extract

zest of 1 orange

150 g (1½ cups) almond meal

60 g (⅓ cup) semolina

2 teaspoons baking powder

½ teaspoon ground cinnamon

Orange Syrup

250 ml (1 cup) orange juice

1 tablespoon lemon juice

60 ml (¼ cup) pure maple syrup

3 whole star anise

2 cinnamon sticks

Serves 12

PREHEAT your oven to 160°C fan-forced. Line a 20 x 10 cm loaf tin with baking paper.

COMBINE eggs, olive oil, sugar, vanilla and orange zest in a large mixing bowl.

ADD the almond meal, semolina, baking powder and cinnamon and mix well to form a smooth batter.

POUR the cake batter into the prepared loaf tin.

BAKE for 45 minutes or until cooked through. Meanwhile, make the Orange Syrup.

To make the Orange Syrup:

COMBINE all ingredients in a saucepan.

SIMMER for 5 minutes over a gentle heat until the syrup has reduced slightly, and the aromatics have infused into the syrup. Remove the star anise and cinnamon sticks.

REMOVE the cake from the oven and pierce all over with a skewer or knife.

POUR the hot syrup over the cake and leave it in the tin for 30 minutes to soak up the syrup.

SERVE at room temperature or chilled and devour.

NOTES AND INSPIRATION

Serve on a platter with orange segments, fresh bay leaves and cinnamon sticks to garnish.

GARDEN ZUCCHINI CAKE

Filled with the goodness of fibre-rich zucchini, this cake is perfect for the whole family. I love that it's not too sweet, and it marries perfectly with omega-3-rich walnuts. I often top it with sliced figs and a little ginger or a drizzle of warmed marmalade.

HIGH FIBRE | LOW GI | VEGETARIAN | GUT FRIENDLY

INGREDIENTS

3 free-range eggs

125 ml (½ cup) pure maple syrup or raw honey

250 ml (1 cup) extra-virgin olive oil

2 teaspoons vanilla extract

2 teaspoons ground ginger

2 teaspoons ground cinnamon

1 tablespoon baking powder

240 g (2 cups) wholemeal spelt flour

500 g zucchini, coarsely grated, moisture squeezed out

155 g (1½ cups) walnuts, chopped

1 quantity Lightened Up Cream Cheese Frosting (p 253) or Lush Ricotta Crème (p 245)

Serves 12

PREHEAT your oven to 160°C fan-forced. Line a 22 cm round cake tin with baking paper.

COMBINE eggs, maple syrup, olive oil, vanilla and spices in a mixing bowl.

ADD baking powder and flour and mix until just combined.

FOLD in the zucchini and walnuts then pour into the tin.

BAKE for 60 minutes and cool.

TOP with Lightened Up Cream Cheese Frosting or Lush Ricotta Crème.

SERVE and enjoy.

NOTES AND INSPIRATION

Decorate with fresh herbs and thin slices of lime to create a beautiful, aromatic centrepiece.

HEALTHY CARROT CAKE

When baking gluten-free cakes, I find almond meal is great. It makes everything so yummy and moist, plus it's packed with protein and vitamin E. I've used a light-flavoured olive oil in this recipe as it gives this cake a luxurious flavour.

GLUTEN-FREE | PROTEIN | SUPERFOOD | LOW GI

INGREDIENTS

500 g carrots, grated

3 free-range eggs

125 ml (½ cup) pure maple syrup or raw honey

60 ml (¼ cup) light-flavoured olive oil

2 teaspoons vanilla extract

300 g (3 cups) almond meal

2 teaspoons ground cinnamon

½ teaspoon nutmeg

2 teaspoons gluten-free baking powder

120 g (¾ cup) raisins

120 g (1¼ cups) walnuts

1 quantity Lightened Up Cream Cheese Frosting (p 253)

Serves 12

PREHEAT your oven to 160°C fan-forced. Lightly grease a 22 cm round cake tin and line with baking paper.

COMBINE carrot, eggs, maple syrup, olive oil, vanilla, almond meal, cinnamon, nutmeg and baking powder in a large bowl.

MIX well by hand until combined. Fold in raisins and walnuts.

POUR into the prepared cake tin.

BAKE for 50 minutes or until cooked through. If necessary, cover with foil to prevent burning.

REMOVE from the oven and allow to cool completely in the tin then turn out.

SPREAD the frosting over the cake and enjoy.

NOTES AND INSPIRATION

Thick Greek or vanilla yoghurt is also a lovely topping for this cake—drizzle with honey and garnish with walnuts or fresh figs. Keeps in the refrigerator for up to 4 days.

BEST-EVER FRUIT CAKE

This is my go-to fruit cake that I make every Christmas. It's naturally sweetened with plump raisins, apricots and orange, and super-moist thanks to the almond meal and olive oil.

GLUTEN-FREE | DAIRY-FREE | STRESS RELIEF

INGREDIENTS

350 g (2⅓ cups) plump raisins

250 g organic apricots, chopped

2 navel oranges

2 teaspoons vanilla extract

1 teaspoon ground cinnamon

1 teaspoon ground ginger

¼ teaspoon ground nutmeg

60 ml (¼ cup) extra-virgin olive oil

60 ml (¼ cup) pure maple syrup

4 large free-range eggs

200 g (2 cups) almond meal

2 teaspoons baking powder

100 g (1 cup) walnuts, chopped

cherries, to garnish (optional)

Serves 12

PREHEAT your oven to 160°C fan-forced. Line a deep 20 cm round cake tin with baking paper.

COMBINE raisins, apricots, zest and juice of 2 oranges, vanilla, cinnamon, ginger, nutmeg, olive oil, maple syrup and eggs.

REST the mixture for 15–30 minutes to allow the fruits to soften.

ADD the almond meal, baking powder and walnuts and mix through.

SPOON into the cake tin.

BAKE for 45–50 minutes or until the cake is cooked through.

COOL and enjoy.

NOTES AND INSPIRATION

Serve topped with fresh cherries, cold or at room temperature. Store in the fridge for up to 2 weeks.

FLOURLESS ORANGE CAKE

Scented with whole sweet navel oranges, vanilla, almonds and honey and topped with caramelised oranges, this is a truly irresistible gluten-free cake that's perfect for any occasion.

PROTEIN | HIGH FIBRE | GLUTEN-FREE

INGREDIENTS

350 g (1–2) whole sweet oranges

3 free-range eggs

125 ml (½ cup) honey

1 teaspoon vanilla extract or paste

200 g (2 cups) almond meal

1 teaspoon baking powder

Caramelised Oranges

2 oranges

2 teaspoons butter

1 teaspoon honey

Serves 10

PREHEAT your oven to 160°C fan-forced. Line a 20 cm round cake tin with baking paper on the base and sides.

STEAM or boil whole oranges for 1 hour until soft. Drain and cool.

ROUGHLY chop cooked oranges and place into a food processor. Process until smooth.

ADD eggs, honey and vanilla then process again until smooth.

ADD almond meal and baking powder then process again.

SPOON cake batter into the tin and smooth over with the back of a spoon.

BAKE for 40–45 minutes or until cooked through and golden.

REMOVE from the oven and allow to cool in the tin for 1 hour before turning out.

To make Caramelised Oranges:

SLICE one orange into even round slices.

ZEST and juice the other orange.

HEAT butter and honey in a large pan until melted and golden. Add the orange slices, juice and zest and heat until golden and caramelised.

REMOVE from the heat and decorate the top of the cake with slices.

POUR the honey caramel sauce over the cake and oranges and enjoy.

NOTES AND INSPIRATION

Pure maple syrup can be used in place of the honey.

FROSTED HUMMINGBIRD CAKE

A luscious cake that's bursting with real fruit goodness! It's loaded with fresh chunks of sunny pineapple and scented with vanilla, capturing the magical essence of a tropical paradise by the ocean.

WELLBEING | WHOLEFOOD | PROBIOTIC

INGREDIENTS

2 medium-sized ripe bananas, mashed

3 free-range eggs

125 ml (½ cup) raw honey

125 ml (½ cup) extra-virgin olive oil or macadamia nut oil

zest of 1 orange

1 teaspoon vanilla extract

3 teaspoons baking powder

240 g (2 cups) spelt flour

100 g (1 cup) desiccated coconut

400 g pineapple, finely chopped

100 g (1 cup) pecans, chopped

2 quantities Yoghurt Frosting or Lightened Up Cream Cheese Frosting (p 253)

passionfruit or mango, to garnish

Serves 16

PREHEAT your oven to 160°C fan-forced. Line two 20 cm round cake tins with baking paper.

COMBINE banana, eggs, honey, olive oil, orange zest, vanilla and baking powder in a large bowl.

ADD spelt flour and coconut and mix through until combined.

FOLD in pineapple and pecan nuts.

DIVIDE the batter between the two tins.

BAKE for about 40 minutes or until cooked through.

REMOVE the cakes from the oven and allow to cool.

SANDWICH the cake with Yoghurt Frosting or Lightened Up Cream Cheese Frosting and ice the top and sides with remaining frosting. Top with passionfruit or mango.

NOTES AND INSPIRATION

Use gluten-free flour in place of the spelt flour for a gluten-free cake. Tinned, chopped pineapple can be used in place of fresh; just drain it before using.

PALEO APPLE CAKE

My great aunt was the queen of apple cakes. I would help her bake the most amazing apple cakes that were jam-packed with seasonal Golden Delicious apples and scented with a hint of vanilla.

GLUTEN-FREE | WELLBEING | GUT FRIENDLY | WHOLEFOOD

INGREDIENTS

200 g (2 cups) almond meal

1 teaspoon gluten-free baking powder

60 ml (¼ cup) extra-virgin olive oil or macadamia nut oil

80 ml (⅓ cup) raw honey

1 teaspoon vanilla extract

2 free-range eggs

zest of 1 orange

2 large red apples, skin on, diced

flaked almonds, to garnish

Serves 8

PREHEAT your oven to 160°C fan-forced. Prepare a 20 cm round cake tin, making sure the base and sides of the tin are lined.

COMBINE almond meal, baking powder, oil, honey, vanilla, eggs and orange zest in a large bowl.

MIX until well combined.

FOLD in the apples.

PRESS the batter firmly into the tin.

GARNISH with flaked almonds.

BAKE for 60–80 minutes.

REST in the tin for 30 minutes before removing.

NOTES AND INSPIRATION

Use pears in place of apples.

LEMON PASSIONFRUIT CHEESECAKE

This is a gluten- and dairy-free treat rich in in fibre, vitamins and restorative minerals. The cashew nuts give this cheesecake a luxurious, creamy texture without the need for dairy or refined sugars.

RAW | PROTEIN | DETOX | DAIRY-FREE | GLUTEN-FREE

INGREDIENTS

140 g (1 cup) almonds

6 fresh dates, pitted

50 g (½ cup) desiccated coconut

pinch of sea salt

Filling

180 g (1½ cups) cashews, soaked for a least 3 hours

185 ml (¾ cup) almond milk

125 ml (½ cup) freshly squeezed lemon juice

60 ml (¼ cup) pure maple syrup

1 teaspoon vanilla extract

125 ml (½ cup) cold-pressed coconut oil

6 passionfruit

Serves 16

LINE a 15 cm springform cake tin with baking paper.

BLITZ almonds, dates, coconut and sea salt in a food processor until the mixture resembles breadcrumbs.

PRESS the almond mixture into the bottom of the tin.

DRAIN the cashews and place in a high-speed blender.

ADD the almond milk, lemon juice, maple syrup and vanilla and blend until smooth and creamy.

ADD coconut oil and blend again until combined.

POUR the creamy filling over the almond crust and level the top.

PLACE the cheesecake in the freezer for 4 hours to set.

REMOVE the cheesecake from the freezer and refrigerate for at least half a day.

GARNISH with passionfruit pulp and enjoy.

NOTES AND INSPIRATION

Top with fresh strawberries in place of passionfruit.

APPLE TEA CAKE

This is a simple and extremely delicious cake to eat. Filled to the brim with finely chopped apples, every mouthful is pure wholesome nourishment.

LOW GI | PLANT-BASED | HIGH FIBRE | GUT FRIENDLY

INGREDIENTS

3 free-range eggs

100 ml extra-virgin olive oil or macadamia nut oil

100 ml pure maple syrup

3 teaspoons baking powder

½ teaspoon ground cinnamon

2 teaspoons vanilla extract

240 g (2 cups) wholemeal spelt flour

750 g Golden Delicious or pink lady apples, skin on, finely diced

Serves 10

PREHEAT your oven to 160°C fan-forced. Line a loaf tin with baking paper.

COMBINE eggs, oil, maple syrup, baking powder, cinnamon and vanilla in a mixing bowl.

ADD spelt flour and mix into a smooth batter.

FOLD in the finely diced apples and mix until all the apples are coated with the batter.

POUR into the loaf tin.

BAKE for 60 minutes until cooked through then remove from the oven to cool.

SERVE warm or at room temperature and enjoy.

NOTES AND INSPIRATION

Use oat flour in place of spelt flour.

APPLE WALNUT CAKE

This is my all-time favourite cake that's wholesome, simple to create and tastes delicious. It's pure comfort food for when it's cold and rainy outside.

LOW SUGAR | WELLBEING | LOW GI

INGREDIENTS

150 g (1 cup) raisins

250 ml (1 cup) hot water

180 ml (¾ cup) extra-virgin olive oil

2 teaspoons vanilla paste

125 ml (½ cup) pure maple syrup

2 free-range eggs

180 g (1½ cups) wholemeal spelt flour

pinch of sea salt

½ teaspoon ground cinnamon

2 teaspoons baking powder

500 g (about 3) pink lady apples, finely diced

125 g (1¼ cups) walnuts, roughly chopped

1 quantity Yoghurt Frosting (p 253), to serve (optional)

Serves 12

PREHEAT your oven to 160°C fan-forced. Line a 20 cm round cake tin with baking paper.

SOAK raisins in the hot water for 15 minutes until softened then drain.

COMBINE olive oil, vanilla, maple syrup and eggs in a mixing bowl.

WHISK until combined and mixture looks creamy.

ADD the flour, salt, cinnamon and baking powder then mix briefly to form a smooth batter.

FOLD in the apples, drained raisins and walnuts.

SPOON into the cake tin.

BAKE for 45–50 minutes.

REMOVE from the oven and cool.

SERVE with or without frosting and enjoy.

NOTES AND INSPIRATION

Add the zest of 1 orange to the mixture.

CIOCIA'S BABKA

Ciocia, my great aunt, would make this cake at least once a week. She would carefully conduct my Uncle Wujek, who mixed it all together using a bowl and a wooden spoon. The wood fire cooked it perfectly.

WELLBEING | LOW GI | WHOLEFOOD

INGREDIENTS

200 g (1¾ cups) spelt flour, plain flour or gluten-free flour

60 g (⅓ cup) cornflour or potato starch

3 teaspoons baking powder

½ teaspoon sea salt

4 large free-range eggs

200 g (1¼ cups) unrefined raw sugar

2 teaspoons vanilla extract

zest and juice of 1 lemon

180 ml (¾ cup) light-flavoured extra-virgin olive oil

250 ml (1 cup) natural yoghurt

icing sugar, to serve

Serves 12

PREHEAT your oven to 160°C fan-forced.

PREPARE a bundt, babka or savarin pan by generously slathering with butter then dusting with flour, breadcrumbs or almond meal so the cake doesn't stick.

COMBINE the flour, cornflour, baking powder and salt in a bowl and set aside.

BEAT the eggs, sugar, vanilla and lemon zest and juice in a bowl of an electric mixer until pale and creamy. Pour in the oil and beat until combined. Add the yoghurt and beat until incorporated into the egg mixture.

ADD the dry ingredients and mix through until you have a thick batter.

POUR the batter into your prepared tin.

BAKE for 40 minutes until cake is cooked through and springs back when touched. Cool for at least 30 minutes in the tin before turning out onto a serving plate.

SERVE with a light dusting of icing sugar.

NOTES AND INSPIRATION

Store in an airtight container for 4 days or refrigerate for 1 week. For a fruity twist, fold a handful of raspberries or blueberries through the batter and drizzle the cake with lemon icing.

PUMPKIN FRUIT CAKE

This nourishing and dense fruit cake uses pumpkin that's full of carotenoids for healthy vision and skin. It's also low GI and low in gluten because of the spelt flour.

WHOLEFOOD | WELLBEING | LOW GI

INGREDIENTS

250 g (2 cups) raw pumpkin, grated

2 free-range eggs

1 teaspoon vanilla extract or paste

60 ml (¼ cup) macadamia nut oil or extra-virgin olive oil

60 ml (¼ cup) raw honey

¾ teaspoon bicarbonate of soda (baking soda)

1 teaspoon ground cinnamon

¼ teaspoon ground nutmeg

¼ teaspoon ground ginger

160 g (1 cup) raisins

120 g (1 cup) wholemeal spelt flour

walnuts or pecans, to garnish (optional)

Serves 14

PREHEAT your oven to 150°C fan-forced. Line a 26 x 10.5 cm loaf tin with baking paper.

COMBINE the raw pumpkin, eggs, vanilla, oil, honey, baking soda, cinnamon, nutmeg, ginger and raisins in a large bowl.

ADD the spelt flour and mix through.

SPOON into the loaf tin.

GARNISH with walnuts or pecans if you desire.

BAKE for 60–75 minutes or until the top of your cake springs back when touched. You may need to cover the top with a little foil to prevent over-browning.

REMOVE from the oven and allow to cool for 30 minutes before removing from the tin.

ENJOY spread with ricotta and a little honey.

NOTES AND INSPIRATION

Use 200 g (2 cups) almond meal in place of wholemeal spelt flour to make it gluten-free.

GLUTEN-FREE CHIFFON CAKE

This will be the lightest and the best sponge cake you've ever made. Take your time and don't rush this recipe—the results are truly worth it. It's perfect on its own or served with semi-whipped Chantilly cream and jam.

GLUTEN-FREE | STRESS RELIEF | GUT FRIENDLY

INGREDIENTS

6 large free-range eggs, separated

pinch of sea salt

200 g (1¼ cups) unrefined raw sugar

60 ml (¼ cup) extra-virgin olive oil

2 teaspoons vanilla extract

120 ml (½ cup) milk, any kind

120 g (¾ cup) rice flour

60 g (⅓ cup) cornflour

2 teaspoons baking powder

Serves 12

PREHEAT your oven to 160°C fan-forced.

WHIP the egg whites with a pinch of salt until soft peaks form, then gradually add the sugar, a little bit at a time. Keep mixing for 6 minutes until stiff peaks form and the whites are glossy.

IN a separate bowl combine the egg yolks, olive oil, vanilla and milk and mix well. Add the rice flour, cornflour and baking powder and mix to form a batter.

FOLD a few spoonfuls of the egg whites into the thick batter. Mix through until combined, folding the mixture with a spoon. Add the rest of the egg whites, carefully folding them through the cake batter.

SPOON the cake mix into a 22 cm non-greased chiffon cake tin.

BAKE for 40–45 minutes until browned and the sponge is cooked. Remove from the oven.

COOL upside down for at least 4 hours until the sponge is completely cold.

CAREFULLY insert a small knife around the sides of the cake to loosen it from the tin. Release the tin from the sponge. Slide a knife through the base of the cake to release the bottom layer from the cake tin.

SERVE the chiffon cake plain or with jam and a little crème fraiche or yoghurt.

NOTES AND INSPIRATION

Use as the perfect base for tiramisu or trifle.

A BETTER PAVLOVA

Made with less sugar than traditional versions, this pavlova will be the hero of your celebration. For the topping, I find mixing together Greek yoghurt and semi-whipped cream produces a lighter, tangier cream that rounds out the sweetness along with the berries.

GLUTEN-FREE | ENERGISING | ALL NATURAL

INGREDIENTS

240 g egg whites (from 6 large eggs), room temperature

380 g (1¾ cups) unrefined raw caster sugar

pinch of sea salt

½ teaspoon cream of tartar

1 tablespoon lemon juice

1 tablespoon cornflour

Topping

250 ml (1 cup) thickened cream

250 ml (1 cup) Greek yoghurt

500 g berries, such as raspberries, blackberries and strawberries

1 tablespoon pure maple syrup

Serves 10

PREHEAT your oven to 150°C, convection (no fan). Line a baking tray with baking paper.

COMBINE the egg whites, sugar, salt and cream of tartar in a bowl of a stand mixer. Sit the bowl over a pan of simmering water (double boiler), making sure that the water does not touch the bottom of the bowl.

HEAT the egg white mixture, stirring with a whisk until the sugar has dissolved and whites are warm to the touch. Your mix should be about 50°C. Transfer the bowl to a stand mixer fitted with the whisk attachment and whip on high speed for 8 minutes, until thick and glossy. Add the lemon juice and cornflour, then mix through.

PILE the meringue onto the baking tray.

SHAPE into a large circle using a palate knife.

PLACE the pavlova in the oven, then immediately reduce the oven temperature to 120°C no-fan.

BAKE for 80 minutes, then turn off the oven and cool completely in the oven with the door closed for 3 hours or overnight.

WHIP the cream until soft peaks form, then gently fold in the yoghurt and spoon over the pavlova. Blend half of the berries with the maple syrup, then mix through the rest of the berries. Spoon the berries over the pavlova and enjoy.

NOTES AND INSPIRATION

You could also top the pavlova with fresh mango and passionfruit.

LEMON YOGHURT CUPCAKES

A light and decadent cupcake that's perfect for an impromptu afternoon tea. It's gluten-free, delicious and perfect served with a dollop of whipped yoghurt or crème fraîche.

WELLBEING | PROTEIN | GLUTEN-FREE

INGREDIENTS

300 g (3 cups) almond meal

2 teaspoons baking powder

zest of 2 lemons

3 large free-range eggs

120 ml (½ cup) raw honey

1 teaspoon vanilla extract

60 ml (¼ cup) light-flavoured extra-virgin olive oil

60 ml (¼ cup) Greek yoghurt

Embellishments (Optional)

Apricot jam, honey, lemon, yoghurt, basil

Makes 12 cupcakes

PREHEAT your oven to 160°C fan-forced. Line a 12-hole cupcake tin with paper cases.

COMBINE almond meal and baking powder in a large bowl. Stir through the lemon zest.

ADD the eggs, honey, vanilla, oil and yoghurt and mix well until combined.

SPOON the mixture into the cupcake cases.

BAKE for 25–30 minutes until cooked through and golden.

REMOVE from the oven and cool completely.

NOTES AND INSPIRATION

Brush the top with a little honey or apricot jam and garnish with fresh lemon. Or add some basil to garnish.

GARDEN OLIVE OIL CAKES

This is the perfect cake that's wonderful to eat with a cup of looseleaf green tea. I love that it's not too sweet and scented with only a hint of raw honey.

GLUTEN-FREE | LOW SUGAR | GUT FRIENDLY | PROTEIN

INGREDIENTS

140 g (1¼ cups) buckwheat flour

100 g (1 cup) almond meal

1 teaspoon bicarbonate of soda (baking soda)

zest of 1 orange

125 ml (½ cup) extra-virgin olive oil

120 ml (½ cup) raw honey

200 ml (¾ cup) natural yoghurt

4 free-range eggs

2 teaspoons vanilla extract

Makes 12 individual cakes or 1 large cake

PREHEAT your oven to 160°C fan-forced.

LINE 12 individual mini cake tins or one 20 cm cake tin. Alternatively, I like to lightly brush the pans with olive oil then dust with almond meal to prevent sticking.

COMBINE buckwheat flour, almond meal and baking soda in a bowl.

ADD orange zest, olive oil, honey, yoghurt, eggs and vanilla.

MIX well with a whisk until combined.

POUR cake batter into the tins.

BAKE for 35–45 minutes or until cooked through.

NOTES AND INSPIRATION

Use apple puree in place of yoghurt to make these cakes dairy-free.

A BEAUTIFUL LEMON CAKE

This is a super-moist gluten-free cake that's not too sweet and perfect for afternoon tea or as dessert at your next dinner party. Enjoy with a glass of Prosecco or chamomile tea.

GLUTEN-FREE | STRESS RELIEF | ALL NATURAL

INGREDIENTS

300 g (3 cups) almond meal

125 ml (½ cup) raw honey

2 teaspoons gluten-free baking powder

½ teaspoon sea salt

4 large free-range eggs

125 ml (½ cup) extra-virgin olive oil

zest and juice of 2 lemons

2 teaspoons vanilla extract

1 quantity Yoghurt Frosting (p 253, optional)

lemon curd, to serve (optional)

Serves 12

PREHEAT your oven to 160°C fan-forced. Line a 20 cm round cake tin with baking paper.

COMBINE almond meal, honey, baking powder, salt, eggs, olive oil, lemon zest and juice and vanilla in a bowl.

MIX well and pour into the prepared tin.

BAKE for 45 minutes until cooked through, then cool.

SERVE the cake simply plain as a tea cake. Alternatively, cut in half and sandwich with Yoghurt Frosting and lemon curd.

ENJOY.

NOTES AND INSPIRATION

Double the recipe and make 2 cakes. Sandwich the cakes with the frosting and lemon curd.

GLUTEN-FREE LAMINGTON CUPCAKES

These cupcakes are a delicious treat packed with protein, healthy fats and vitamin E for glowing skin. Topped with my luscious, lightened-up cream cheese frosting that brings all the fun without the guilt, they're a sweet indulgence your body (and taste buds) will love.

PROTEIN | GLUTEN-FREE

INGREDIENTS

300 g (3 cups) almond meal

75 g (1 cup) desiccated coconut

2½ teaspoons gluten-free baking powder

80 ml (⅓ cup) olive oil

80 ml (⅓ cup) raw honey or pure maple syrup

4 large free-range eggs

1 teaspoon vanilla extract

pinch sea salt

125 ml (½ cup) almond milk or coconut milk

1 quantity Lightened Up Cream Cheese Frosting (p 253)

Embellishments

Raspberries, chopped white chocolate, cocoa powder, matcha powder, coconut flakes

Makes 12 cupcakes

PREHEAT your oven to 160°C fan-forced. Line a 12-hole cupcake tin with paper cases.

COMBINE almond meal, coconut and baking powder in a large bowl.

ADD the olive oil, honey or maple syrup, eggs, vanilla and salt.

POUR in the milk and mix to make a smooth batter. At this stage you can also fold in a handful of raspberries or white chocolate chunks for that lamington vibe.

SPOON lamington cupcake batter into the prepared tin.

BAKE for 35–40 minutes or until cooked through and golden. Remove from the oven and cool completely.

APPLY generous amounts of frosting to each lamington cupcake.

TOP with your choice of embellishments and store in the fridge until required.

NOTES AND INSPIRATION

Add the zest of 1 orange and use orange juice in place of almond milk.

CHOCOLATE LOVE

HEALTHY CHOCOLATE ÉCLAIRS

Éclairs add a decadent touch to any afternoon tea. They're best made with spelt or all-purpose plain flour, however they will also work well with gluten-free flour. Fill with your choice of custard or whipped ricotta.

HIGH FIBRE | PROTEIN | WELLBEING

INGREDIENTS

125 ml (½ cup) water

50 g (¼ cup) butter

pinch of salt

100 g spelt flour, plain flour or gluten-free flour

3 free-range eggs

1 teaspoon baking powder

1 quantity Lush Ricotta Crème (p 245) or Vanilla Crème Patissiere (p 242)

1 quantity Dark Chocolate Ganache (p 245)

Makes 24 éclairs

PREHEAT your oven to 180°C fan-forced and line a baking tray with baking paper.

COMBINE water, butter and salt in a heavy-based pan and bring to a gentle simmer until the butter melts.

ADD the flour, stirring vigorously with a wooden spoon for 1–2 minutes until you achieve a soft playdough-like mass. Cook for a few seconds until the dough pulls away from the pot, then remove from the heat.

ADD eggs one at a time, incorporating each egg completely before adding the next. Check the dough after two eggs then add the third egg. You can do this directly in the pan or transfer the dough to a stand mixer. Add the baking powder last.

FILL a pastry bag fitted with a plain nozzle and pipe into 5 cm lengths onto the prepared baking tray.

BAKE for 30 minutes until puffed and golden and allow to cool completely.

CUT a slit into the side of each éclair and fill with your choice of pastry crème. Spread ganache over éclairs and place onto a tray to set.

NOTES AND INSPIRATION

Decorate with superfoods such as bee pollen, roasted hazelnuts, freeze-dried raspberries or pistachio nuts. A little gold leaf looks spectacular.

RED VELVET CUPCAKES

This is my healthy take on the traditional red velvet chocolate cake. These cupcakes are lovely and moist from the fresh grated beetroot that I've added into my batter, replacing the traditional red food colouring found in most recipes. The finished cupcakes look wholesome and taste delicious.

PROTEIN | SUPERFOOD | GLUTEN-FREE | LOW GI

INGREDIENTS

260 g (about 2 large) beetroots, skin on, grated

2 free-range eggs

1 teaspoon vanilla paste

½ teaspoon ground cinnamon

pinch of sea salt

150 g (1½ cups) almond meal

3 tablespoons cocoa powder or Healthy Chef Naked Chocolat

60 ml (¼ cup) honey or pure maple syrup

3 tablespoons olive oil

1 teaspoon gluten-free baking powder (or ¼ teaspoon bicarbonate of soda)

½ cup frozen raspberries

Makes 12 cupcakes

PREHEAT your oven to 160°C fan-forced. Line a 12-hole muffin tin with paper cases.

COMBINE grated beetroot, eggs, vanilla, cinnamon, salt, almond meal, cocoa, honey, olive oil and baking powder in a large bowl.

MIX well with your hands until combined.

FOLD through the raspberries.

SPOON into the muffin cases.

BAKE for 45 minutes or until cooked through.

REMOVE from the oven and cool completely in the tin.

SERVE topped with vanilla frosting (see Notes) or Greek yoghurt.

NOTES AND INSPIRATION

To make vanilla frosting combine 250 g quark or labneh with 2 tablespoons honey and 1 teaspoon vanilla paste. Mix well until combined.

CHOCOLATE AND BANANA BREAD

One can never have too many banana bread recipes! This chocolate banana bread is naturally gluten-free and rich in antioxidants, heart-healthy fats and fibre, supporting sustained energy, gut health and overall wellbeing. Enjoy a slice when you feel like a little chocolate therapy.

GLUTEN-FREE | GUT FRIENDLY | HIGH FIBRE

INGREDIENTS

300 g (about 3) bananas, mashed, plus 1 extra to garnish

80 ml (⅓ cup) pure maple syrup

125 ml (½ cup) almond milk

125 ml (½ cup) extra-virgin olive oil

2 teaspoons vanilla extract

1 teaspoon sea salt

120 g (1¼ cups) almond meal

60 g (½ cup) cocoa powder

70 g (½ cup) buckwheat flour

3 teaspoons gluten-free baking powder

Makes 1 loaf

PREHEAT oven to 160°C fan-forced. Line a loaf tin with baking paper.

COMBINE banana, maple syrup, almond milk, olive oil, vanilla and salt in a blender and puree until smooth.

POUR into a mixing bowl.

ADD the almond meal, cocoa, buckwheat flour and baking powder and mix well.

POUR into the loaf tin. Garnish with a banana, sliced in half lengthwise.

BAKE for 50–60 minutes until cooked through.

COOL and devour.

NOTES AND INSPIRATION

Serve alone or topped with natural Greek yoghurt. Perfect with a cup of filter coffee or espresso.

WORLD'S HEALTHIEST CHOCOLATE CAKE

This chocolate cake is brimming with antioxidants to boost energy and promote wellbeing. I love that it's super-moist and rich in heart-healthy essential fats from the avocado oil. This cake is gluten-free, dairy-free and refined sugar-free, making it the perfect healthy treat for everyone.

GLUTEN-FREE | DAIRY-FREE | LOW GI | STRESS RELIEF

INGREDIENTS

125 ml (½ cup) extra-virgin avocado or olive oil

125 ml (½ cup) almond milk

125 ml (½ cup) maple syrup

4 free-range eggs

2 teaspoons vanilla extract

3 teaspoons gluten-free baking powder

60 g (½ cup) dark cocoa powder

300 g (3 cups) almond meal

Avocado Frosting

2 ripe avocados, skin and stone removed

125 ml (½ cup) maple syrup

125 ml (½ cup) coconut cream or yoghurt

2 teaspoons vanilla extract

60 g (½ cup) dark cocoa powder

pinch of sea salt

Makes 1 single layer cake

PREHEAT your oven to 160°C fan-forced. Line 22 cm round cake tin with baking paper.

COMBINE oil, almond milk, maple syrup, eggs and vanilla in a bowl.

ADD the baking powder, cocoa and almond meal and mix through until combined.

POUR the mixture into the cake tin.

BAKE for 45 minutes until cooked then remove from the oven to cool.

COMBINE all frosting ingredients in a blender and blend until smooth. Ice the cake generously.

STORE in the fridge until ready to serve.

NOTES AND INSPIRATION

Double the recipe if making a double layered cake with frosting as pictured.

NAKED CHOCOLATE CAKE

This delicious cake can be enjoyed by everyone. A wonderful gluten-free, one-bowl chocolate cake that's nut-free and kind to sensitive digestive systems.

PALEO | GRAIN-FREE | WELLBEING | GLUTEN-FREE

INGREDIENTS

12 free-range eggs

125 ml (½ cup) raw honey

2 teaspoons vanilla paste or extract

½ teaspoon sea salt

250 ml (1 cup) extra-virgin olive oil or coconut oil

120 g (1 cup) cocoa powder

130 g (1 cup) coconut flour

1 tablespoon gluten-free baking powder

250 ml (1 cup) coconut milk

Makes 1 large or 2 smaller cakes

PREHEAT your oven to 160°C fan-forced. Line two 15 cm round cake tins or one 20 cm round cake tin with baking paper.

BEAT eggs for 10 minutes using the whisk attachment of your stand mixer until creamy.

ADD honey, vanilla and sea salt and continue to whisk for another 5 minutes.

ADD olive oil and mix through quickly then add the cocoa powder, coconut flour, baking powder and coconut milk.

MIX until well combined.

POUR into the two cake tins.

BAKE the cakes for 35–40 minutes or until cooked through.

REMOVE from the oven and cool.

SANDWICH the two chocolate cakes with your choice of frosting.

NOTES AND INSPIRATION

Top with whipped coconut cream or yoghurt and drizzle with smashed raspberry puree.

FLOURLESS SALTED CHOCOLATE CAKE

The cacao in dark chocolate is rich in magnesium, iron, copper, manganese, riboflavin and essential micronutrients for health and vitality. The high flavonoid content of cacao has been scientifically linked to a reduced risk of heart disease, stroke and diabetes. Cacao contains theobromine, which boosts endorphins and increases mental alertness.

PROTEIN | GLUTEN-FREE | LOW GI

INGREDIENTS

200 g good-quality 70% dark eating chocolate

175 g good-quality butter

6 free-range eggs, at room temperature

2 tablespoons coconut sugar, raw sugar or honey

2 teaspoons natural vanilla extract or paste

good pinch of sea salt

Serves 20

PREHEAT your oven to 150°C fan-forced.

LIGHTLY oil or butter a cake tin and line completely with baking paper. I use a 20 cm springform cake tin for this recipe.

MELT the dark chocolate and butter in a bowl set over a pan of gently simmering water.

STIR the chocolate and butter well until melted then remove from heat and allow to cool slightly.

USING a stand mixer fitted with a wire whisk, beat eggs for 10–15 minutes until light and creamy.

ADD coconut sugar, vanilla and sea salt and beat until combined.

FOLD half of the melted chocolate mixture through the beaten eggs and incorporate lightly. Then add the rest of the melted chocolate and fold through gently until combined.

POUR the mixture into the prepared baking tin.

BAKE the cake for 35 minutes or until just set and springs back lightly when touched.

REMOVE from the oven and allow to cool.

PLACE the cake in the refrigerator to cool completely before removing from the tin.

SERVE and enjoy. Store in the refrigerator.

NOTES AND INSPIRATION

Serve with fresh raspberries.

THE ONLY CHOCOLATE CAKE YOU'LL EVER NEED

This easy flourless chocolate cake is sure to please. It's not too sweet so it's perfect served at your next celebration or dinner party.

WELLBEING | GRAIN-FREE | GLUTEN-FREE | PALEO

INGREDIENTS

125 ml (½ cup) olive oil

125 g good-quality 70% dark eating chocolate, melted

100 g (½ cup) coconut sugar

3 large free-range eggs

1 teaspoon vanilla extract

125 g (1¼ cups) almond meal

2 teaspoons baking powder

2 tablespoons coffee powder, optional

Embellishments

Ganache, mascarpone, blackberries, raspberries, icing sugar

Serves 14

PREHEAT your oven to 160°C fan-forced. Line a 20 cm round cake tin with baking paper.

POUR the olive oil into the melted chocolate and mix until combined.

ADD the coconut sugar and whisk, followed by the eggs and vanilla. Mix in the almond meal and baking powder and coffee powder, if using.

SPOON the batter into the prepared cake tin.

BAKE for 30 minutes until the cake is set on top. The inside will still be slightly moist. Cool in the tin for 30 minutes before turning out to cool completely.

SERVE by itself or topped with your choice of embellishments.

NOTES AND INSPIRATION

Store in the fridge for up to 5 days.

FLOURLESS CHOCOLATE BROWNIE

This is my secret brownie recipe from when I had The Healthy Chef Cafe. It's one of the most requested recipes on my blog and I was compelled to add this one into the mix.

GLUTEN-FREE | PROTEIN | ANTIOXIDANTS | PALEO

INGREDIENTS

200 g butter

200 g good-quality 70% dark eating chocolate, chopped

3 free-range eggs

60 ml (¼ cup) raw honey or pure maple syrup

60 g (½ cup) coconut flour

150 g (1½ cups) walnuts

Makes 40 small slices

PREHEAT your oven to 180°C fan-forced. Line a 22.5 cm square cake tin with baking paper.

MELT butter in a saucepan over a very low heat.

REMOVE from the heat and add chocolate to the saucepan.

MIX in the chocolate until it has melted through.

ADD eggs and honey and combine.

STIR in coconut flour and fold in the walnuts.

POUR brownie mixture into the prepared tin.

BAKE for 20 minutes and remove from the oven. The brownie will still be soft and fudge-like.

COOL to room temperature then place in the fridge to set.

CUT into small fingers and serve.

NOTES AND INSPIRATION

Use cold-pressed coconut oil in place of butter, but be careful not to overheat when melting.

VEGAN CHOCOLATE SWEET POTATO BROWNIES

Sweet potatoes are high in betacarotene, which your body converts to vitamin A, which helps protect against free radicals, promotes healthy skin and supports your immune system.

GLUTEN-FREE | ENERGISING | ANTIOXIDANTS

INGREDIENTS

500 g sweet potato, roasted and mashed

12 soft fresh dates, pitted

125 ml (½ cup) extra-virgin olive oil

60 ml (¼ cup) pure maple syrup

2 teaspoons vanilla extract

100 g (1 cup) dark cocoa powder

200 g (2 cups) almond meal

3 tablespoons tapioca flour

1 teaspoon gluten-free baking powder

pinch of sea salt

Serves 16

PREHEAT your oven to 160°C fan-forced. Line a baking dish with baking paper.

COMBINE sweet potatoes, dates, olive oil, maple syrup and vanilla in a food processor.

BLEND until all the ingredients have combined to a smooth, silky paste.

ADD the cocoa powder, almond meal, tapioca flour, baking powder and salt.

BLEND again until all the dry ingredients have combined with the sweet potato mixture.

SPOON into the baking dish.

BAKE for 45 minutes then remove from the oven.

COOL in the baking dish and refrigerate for 4 hours to firm up; I like to do this overnight for best results.

CUT the brownie into small portions to serve.

NOTES AND INSPIRATION

Store these brownies in the fridge for up to 5 days or freeze.

OMG CHOCOLATE CUPCAKES

'OMG' was the first word that came out of my husband's mouth after he took a bite of these little cakes. Super-moist and easy to make, this recipe can be made as cupcakes or as a whole cake. Don't over bake them—they're actually best slightly under baked, which makes them fudgy inside.

GLUTEN-FREE | ALL NATURAL

INGREDIENTS

1 quantity Dark Chocolate Ganache (p 245)

250 ml (1 cup) hot water from a recently boiled kettle

120 g (⅔ cup) coconut sugar

60 g (½ cup) dark cocoa powder

125 ml (½ cup) extra-virgin olive oil

2 large free-range eggs

1 teaspoon vanilla extract

180 g (1½ cups) gluten-free flour or spelt flour

2 teaspoons gluten-free baking powder

1 teaspoon sea salt

Makes 12 cupcakes

MAKE the Dark Chocolate Ganache the day before.

NEXT day, preheat your oven to 160°C fan-forced. Line a muffin or cupcake tin with paper cases.

COMBINE hot water, coconut sugar and cocoa powder in a bowl.

ADD the olive oil, eggs and vanilla and whisk well until combined.

STIR through the flour, baking powder and salt.

SPOON the batter into the prepared tin.

BAKE for 25–30 minutes, then remove from the oven and cool.

FROST with ganache and enjoy.

NOTES AND INSPIRATION

For a special touch, pipe the ganache onto each cupcake using a disposable piping bag fitted with a star tube. Serve with blackberries on the side.

SUPERFOOD CHOCOLATE TART

A quick and easy raw chocolate tart that's perfect for any occasion. Avocado is my favourite anti-ageing superfood because it's full of antioxidants that help nourish healthy glowing skin.

SUPERFOOD | GUT FRIENDLY | VEGAN

INGREDIENTS

Base

250 g (2½ cups) almond meal

4 heaped tablespoons raw cacao powder

½ teaspoon ground cinnamon

pinch of sea salt

6 fresh dates, pitted

3 tablespoons cold-pressed coconut oil

1 teaspoon vanilla extract

Filling

4 ripe medium-sized avocados, skin and stone removed

4 tablespoons raw honey

60 ml (¼ cup) coconut milk or yoghurt

125 ml (½ cup) cold-pressed coconut oil, solid form

1 teaspoon vanilla extract

pinch of sea salt

60 g (½ cup) cacao powder

bee pollen, cacao nibs or raspberries, to garnish (optional)

Serves 12

LINE a springform tart tin.

COMBINE almond meal, cacao, cinnamon and salt in a food processor. Add the dates and blitz through the almond meal until combined. Add the coconut oil and vanilla and blitz again until you have a soft, chocolatey dough.

TRANSFER the dough to the prepared tart tin and press out over the base and sides of the tin.

REFRIGERATE or freeze for 1 hour.

COMBINE avocado, honey, coconut milk, oil, vanilla, salt and cacao in a high-speed blender and blend until smooth and creamy.

POUR the filling mixture over the nut base.

GARNISH with bee pollen, cacao nibs or raspberries if desired.

REFRIGERATE for 2–3 hours before serving.

NOTES AND INSPIRATION

Add the zest of 1 orange to the avocado filling for a jaffa flavour.

PIES, TARTS + CRUMBLES

GLUTEN-FREE APPLE CRUMBLE

This crumble is filled with fibre and naturally sweetened with juicy pink lady apples that have a slight tartness and hold their shape without going mushy. It's perfect for the whole family and your body will thank you for it.

GLUTEN-FREE | HIGH FIBRE | ENERGISING

INGREDIENTS

6 pink lady apples, skin on, chopped

zest and juice of 1 orange

juice of 1 lemon

1 teaspoon vanilla extract

2 tablespoons pure maple syrup

60 ml (¼ cup) water

The Perfect Custard (p 241) or Greek yoghurt, to serve

Crumble

100 g (1 cup) almond meal

100 g (⅔ cup) rice flour

90 g (½ cup) unrefined raw sugar or coconut sugar

100 g butter, room temperature

zest of 1 orange

Serves 6

PREHEAT your oven to 180°C fan-forced.

COMBINE the apples, orange zest and juice, lemon juice, vanilla, maple syrup and water in a large, heavy-based pan.

COVER and cook over medium heat for 6–8 minutes, stirring occasionally until the apples have softened and collapsed. Remove the lid and allow some of the excess liquid to evaporate. You want the apples to be in a lovely citrusy sauce. Taste and adjust the sweetness to your liking.

COMBINE the crumble ingredients in a bowl and set aside.

PILE the apple mixture into a suitably sized baking dish.

SCATTER the crumble generously over the top.

BAKE for 20–25 minutes or until the crumble is golden.

REMOVE from the oven and serve with The Perfect Custard or Greek yoghurt.

NOTES AND INSPIRATION

Fold through a punnet of blackberries before baking.

RHUBARB AND CUSTARD

The magnificent tart flavour of rhubarb dances on the taste buds and makes for perfect comfort food. Rhubarb is high in antioxidants and is wonderful for digestive health.

GLUTEN-FREE | PLANT-BASED | PROTEIN | GUT FRIENDLY

INGREDIENTS

1 bunch rhubarb, leaves discarded, stems washed and chopped

3 tablespoons Pedro Ximénez sherry

2 tablespoons pure maple syrup

2 teaspoons vanilla extract

The Perfect Custard (p 241), to serve

Crumble (Optional)

155 g (1½ cups) almond meal

2 tablespoons extra-virgin olive oil

2 tablespoons pure maple syrup

Serves 6

PREHEAT your oven to 160°C fan-forced.

COMBINE rhubarb, sherry, maple syrup and vanilla in a baking dish.

BAKE for 20 minutes until soft then remove from the oven.

IF USING CRUMBLE, mix together the crumble ingredients and bake separately in a baking dish for 15–20 minutes until golden.

SERVE rhubarb topped with custard and crumble.

ENJOY.

NOTES AND INSPIRATION

Add a handful of raspberries to the rhubarb before cooking for a richer colour.

RHUBARB RASPBERRY CRUMBLE

A truly heavenly crumble that's perfect on cold, rainy nights. Any leftovers can be enjoyed for breakfast the next morning with a dollop of cultured Greek yoghurt.

GUT FRIENDLY | HIGH FIBRE | WELLBEING

INGREDIENTS

Crumble

100 g (1 cup) almond meal

50 g (½ cup) rolled oats

80 g butter, room temperature

2 tablespoons unrefined raw sugar or coconut sugar

Rhubarb Raspberry Filling

1 bunch (400 g) rhubarb, washed, trimmed and cut into chunks

juice of 1 orange (about ½ cup)

1 teaspoon vanilla paste

2 tablespoons pure maple syrup or raw honey

½ cup raspberries, fresh or frozen

Serves 6–8

PREHEAT your oven to 180°C fan-forced.

COMBINE crumble ingredients in a mixing bowl and rub with your fingers until the mixture is crumbly. Set aside.

To make the filling:

COMBINE rhubarb, orange juice, vanilla and maple syrup in a bowl, then transfer to a baking dish.

ROAST rhubarb for 15 minutes.

SCATTER the raspberries over the rhubarb mixture and gently fold through.

TOP rhubarb filling with the crumble.

BAKE for a further 20 minutes or until golden and enjoy.

NOTES AND INSPIRATION

Use freshly brewed rosehip and hibiscus tea in place of orange juice.

PLUM AND HAZELNUT CRUMBLE

A warming dessert with aromatics of red wine, cinnamon and vanilla. Plums are high in potassium, a mineral that helps support healthy blood pressure, and fibre for great digestive health.

WELLBEING | HIGH FIBRE | LOW GI | GLUTEN-FREE

INGREDIENTS

8 plums, halved and stoned

500 ml (2 cups) red wine

1 teaspoon vanilla extract

60 ml (¼ cup) pure maple syrup

3 cinnamon sticks

2 star anise

Greek yoghurt, ricotta or mascarpone, to serve

Hazelnut Crumble

50 g (⅔ cup) hazelnuts

100 g (1 cup) almond or hazelnut meal

2 tablespoons unrefined raw sugar or coconut sugar

50 g butter, room temperature, or 2½ tablespoons extra-virgin olive oil

Serves 6–8

PREHEAT your oven to 160°C fan-forced and line a baking tray with baking paper.

ARRANGE plums in a baking dish or cast-iron pan.

COMBINE red wine, vanilla, maple syrup, cinnamon and star anise in a bowl, then pour over the plums.

BAKE for 30 minutes until plums are soft and wine has thickened slightly.

To make the crumble:

COMBINE hazelnuts, almond meal, sugar and butter or oil in a bowl, mixing with your fingers until the mixture resembles breadcrumbs.

SCATTER onto the prepared baking tray and bake for 10–15 minutes until golden.

SERVE plums topped with the crumble, along with thick Greek yoghurt, ricotta or mascarpone.

NOTES AND INSPIRATION

The roasted plums in red wine make a spectacular whole fruit jam that's perfect over wholegrain sourdough and ricotta.

WHOLESOME APPLE PIE

This spectacular pie is packed with delicious, fibre-rich apples to support digestion and cardiovascular health. The crust is made with my foolproof pastry dough that has been lightly sweetened and rolled with oatmeal.

HIGH FIBRE | WELLBEING | GUT FRIENDLY

INGREDIENTS

8 sweet red apples or Golden Delicious apples

125 ml (½ cup) fresh apple juice

2 teaspoons vanilla extract or paste

½ teaspoon ground cinnamon

1–2 tablespoons pure maple syrup

1 quantity Foolproof Pastry (p 237)

Serves 6–8

QUARTER the apples and remove the core. Cut each quarter in half and place in a large saucepan with the apple juice, vanilla and cinnamon. Cook over a medium heat until soft. Cool, drain off any excess liquid and fold in the maple syrup.

PREHEAT your oven to 180°C fan-forced.

ROLL two-thirds of your chilled pastry between 2 sheets of baking paper to fit a 20 cm pie dish.

LINE the pie dish evenly and fill in any gaps in the pastry as needed.

SPOON in the cold apple filling.

ROLL out the rest of the pastry and gently place over the apple filling. Seal the edges and cut a small slit at the top to allow air to escape.

BAKE for 45 minutes or until golden.

NOTES AND INSPIRATION

Serve warm or at room temperature with custard, yoghurt or ice-cream.

BLUEBERRY GALETTE

You can use a good-quality store-bought all-butter shortcrust or puff pastry to make this recipe if you don't want to make your own. The galette is easy to put together and it looks spectacular when you pull it out of the oven. Best eaten on the day it's baked.

ANTIOXIDANTS | ENERGISING | ALL NATURAL

INGREDIENTS

1 quantity Foolproof Pastry (p 237)

800 g blueberries

3 tablespoons blueberry jam

3 tablespoons cornflour

2 tablespoons lemon juice

yoghurt gelato or crème fraiche, to serve

Serves 12

PREHEAT your oven to 180°C fan-forced and line a baking tray with baking paper.

ROLL the pastry between 2 sheets of baking paper into a 35 cm circle and place on the prepared baking tray.

COMBINE the blueberries, jam, cornflour and lemon juice in a bowl, then pile over the centre of the pastry circle, leaving a 3–4 cm border.

ENCLOSE the edges of the pastry, folding the pastry border over the fruit, so that the blueberries stay intact.

BRUSH with milk or a beaten egg and sprinkle the edges of the pastry with a little raw sugar.

BAKE for 40–45 minutes or until the galette is cooked. I love it when the juices are bubbling and oozing out of the tart.

SERVE with yoghurt gelato or crème fraiche.

NOTES AND INSPIRATION

Use blackberries in place of blueberries.

PEARS POACHED IN WINE

Pears and wine are a match made in heaven. A good resveratrol-rich pinot or herbaceous, French-style, dry vermouth are my absolute favourites. Serve alongside a creamy burrata or a dollop of whipped ricotta.

GLUTEN-FREE | PROTEIN | HIGH FIBRE | WELLBEING

INGREDIENTS

1 bottle of good-quality pinot

250 ml (1 cup) water

125 ml (½ cup) raw honey, pure maple syrup or raw sugar

2 teaspoons vanilla extract

3 cinnamon sticks

6 Beurré Bosc pears, peeled

burrata, to serve

Serves 6

COMBINE wine, water, honey, vanilla and cinnamon in a saucepan and bring to a simmer.

ADD the pears and cover with a lid or cartouche of baking paper.

SIMMER on a gentle heat for 30 minutes until pears are just tender but still holding their shape.

REMOVE the pears from the liquid and set aside in a bowl.

REDUCE the poaching liquid by half until syrupy and gorgeous, then pour the syrup over the pears.

CHILL the pears in the wine syrup until ready to serve.

SERVE pears alongside burrata and enjoy.

NOTES AND INSPIRATION

Burrata is a creamy cow's milk cheese of mozzarella, filled with a lush cream inside the mozzarella skin. Pierce the skin so the cream spills out, creating a spectacular sauce that goes with just about anything sweet or savoury.

PEAR AND ALMOND TART

A classic French tart filled with almond and vanilla-scented frangipane. I've made this recipe using poached pears, but it also works exceptionally well with fresh apricots or blueberries. Serve at your next dinner party and enjoy with a dollop of Greek yoghurt.

GLUTEN-FREE | HIGH FIBRE | WELLBEING

INGREDIENTS

250 g butter, room temperature

160 g (1 cup) unrefined raw sugar

2 teaspoons vanilla extract

250 g (2½ cups) almond meal

40 g (⅓ cup) cornflour or potato starch

2 large free-range eggs

6–8 poached pear halves, drained

2 tablespoons flaked almonds, to garnish (optional)

2 tablespoons pure maple syrup or apricot jam, to glaze

Serves 12

PREHEAT your oven to 180°C fan-forced. Line a round 20 cm or 22 cm cake tin with baking paper.

BEAT the butter, sugar and vanilla in a bowl until creamy.

ADD the almond meal, cornflour and eggs and mix well.

SPOON the mixture into the cake tin, spreading it evenly over the base.

ARRANGE the pear halves over the almond tart mixture.

DECORATE with flaked almonds if desired.

BAKE the tart for 45–50 minutes, or until golden and firm to touch.

COOL completely before removing it from the tin.

GLAZE with warmed apricot jam.

SERVE at room temperature.

NOTES AND INSPIRATION

You can use homemade poached pears or store-bought pear halves in natural juice.

RUSTIC STRAWBERRY GALETTE

This French-inspired tart looks like a Picasso masterpiece when it's pulled out of the oven, with its golden, flaky pastry surrounding a generous filling of juicy strawberries. Serve at your next celebration alongside lashings of probiotic-rich Greek yoghurt or kefir.

ENERGISING | ANTIOXIDANTS | WELLBEING

INGREDIENTS

1 quantity Foolproof Pastry (p 237)

3 tablespoons of good-quality strawberry jam

750 g strawberries, stems removed and halved

2 generous tablespoons raw sugar

1 generous tablespoon cornflour

1 teaspoon vanilla extract

Serves 12

PREHEAT your oven to 200°C fan-forced.

ROLL the dough out between 2 sheets of baking paper to form a circle about 35 cm in diameter.

TRANSFER the dough onto a baking tray and spread over a little jam, leaving a 3 cm border around the edges.

MIX the strawberries with the sugar, cornflour and vanilla.

PILE the strawberries on the pastry, leaving a 3 cm border.

FOLD the edge of the pastry over to enclose the strawberries.

BAKE for 45 minutes until the pastry is golden.

COOL for 10 minutes before devouring.

NOTES AND INSPIRATION

Serve with yoghurt and crème fraiche.

PEACH AND RASPBERRY CRUMBLE

An antioxidant-rich crumble that's delicious topped with thick coconut or Greek yoghurt. Enjoy the leftovers for breakfast by blending it up for a power smoothie.

SUPERFOOD | ANTI-AGEING | RAW | GLUTEN-FREE

INGREDIENTS

80 g (½ cup) dry roasted or raw almonds

½ teaspoon ground cinnamon

4 fresh Medjool dates, pitted

200 g raspberries (if using frozen, defrost first)

2 teaspoons raw honey

juice of 1 orange

3 large yellow peaches

Serves 3–4

COMBINE almonds, cinnamon and dates in a food processor and process until the mixture resembles breadcrumbs.

SMASH raspberries with the honey and orange juice.

CUT peaches in half and remove the stone.

ARRANGE the peaches in a serving dish.

SPOON over the smashed raspberries.

SCATTER the almond crumble mix over the peaches.

SERVE immediately and enjoy.

NOTES AND INSPIRATION

Use other fruits and nuts for variation. Try figs, white peaches and strawberries.

APPLE AND MAPLE TARTE TATIN

Start preparing this tart one hour before your friends pop over for dinner. Put on some French music, have a glass of rosé with your partner and feel the joy this luscious dessert creates in the home. Use a good store-bought butter puff pastry if you don't want to make your own.

ALL NATURAL | ENERGISING | STRESS RELIEF

INGREDIENTS

125 ml (½ cup) pure maple syrup

30 g good-quality butter

8 pink lady apples, peeled, cored and cut in half

1 orange or lemon

1 quantity Spelt Rough Puff Pastry (p 237) or store-bought butter puff pastry

burrata, semi-whipped cream or Greek yoghurt, to serve

Serves 12

PREHEAT your oven to 180°C fan-forced.

CARAMELISE the maple syrup in a large 23 cm cast-iron frying pan for 5 minutes, until it starts to get thick and syrupy.

STIR through the butter until melted and then turn off the heat.

ARRANGE the apple halves, packing them tightly into the pan cut-side up, starting around the edges and working your way inside. Make sure there are no gaps.

GRATE over the zest of 1 orange or lemon and squeeze half of the juice over the apples.

ROLL the pastry into a large 30 cm circle, about 3 mm thick. Lay the pastry on top of the apples.

TUCK in the edges neatly and brush the top of the pastry with a little beaten egg or milk.

BAKE the tart in the oven for 50–60 minutes until the pastry is a rich golden brown.

COOL for about 5 minutes before turning, apple-side up, onto the serving plate.

ENJOY and devour with your choice of burrata, semi-whipped cream or Greek yoghurt.

NOTES AND INSPIRATION

Use pears or other fruits in place of apples. Add a splash of calvados to the apples before baking.

PIES, TARTS + CRUMBLES

RUSTIC PLUM TART

This is a very impressive dessert that will wow your friends when it comes out of the oven. Serve warm or at room temperature with a dollop of yoghurt, crème fraiche or gelato.

ALL NATURAL | ENERGISING | STRESS RELIEF

INGREDIENTS

1 quantity Foolproof Pastry (p 237)

3 tablespoons plum or apricot jam

30 g (¼ cup) almond meal

pinch of ground cinnamon

800 g ripe plums, pitted and cut into quarters

milk or egg wash

2 tablespoons butter

Greek yoghurt, labneh or crème fraiche, to serve

Serves 12

PREHEAT your oven to 200°C fan-forced. Line a baking tray with baking paper.

ROLL the pastry dough between 2 sheets of baking paper into a 35 cm circle.

SPREAD the pastry with the plum jam, leaving a 3 cm border around the edge, and sprinkle over almond meal and a little cinnamon.

ARRANGE the plums over the pastry, leaving a generous 3–4 cm border on the outside.

FOLD the pastry to enclose the plums and brush the outer edges with a little milk or egg wash. Dot butter on top of the plums.

BAKE for 40–45 minutes or until the pastry is golden and the plums have collapsed.

REMOVE from the oven and cool for 5 minutes.

SERVE warm alongside thick Greek yoghurt, labneh or crème fraiche.

NOTES AND INSPIRATION

Use quince paste in place of plum jam. If you want to save time, use a good-quality store-bought, all-butter shortcrust or puff pastry instead of making your own.

MUFFINS + SCONES

OATMEAL, PEAR AND VANILLA MUFFINS

Oats are a delicious source of beta-glucan fibre, which can help lower cholesterol naturally and improve digestion. To make your own oat flour, just blend oats in a food processor or blender until finely ground.

VEGETARIAN | LOW GI | HIGH FIBRE | GUT FRIENDLY

INGREDIENTS

500 g pears, skin on, finely chopped, plus 1 pear, thinly sliced, to garnish

80 ml (⅓ cup) extra-virgin olive oil

60 ml (¼ cup) pure maple syrup or raw honey

3 free-range eggs

1 teaspoon ground cinnamon

1 teaspoon vanilla extract

220 g (1¾ cups) oat flour

Makes 6 large or 12 small muffins

PREHEAT your oven to 160°C fan-forced. Line a muffin tin with paper cases. You can make 6 large or 12 small muffins.

COMBINE chopped pears, olive oil, maple syrup, eggs, cinnamon and vanilla in a bowl.

ADD the oat flour and fold through with a spoon until mixed through.

SPOON batter into the prepared muffin tin using an ice-cream scoop for easier portioning—otherwise use a spoon. Top each muffin with a thin slice of pear.

BAKE for approximately 40–45 minutes until cooked through.

COOL in the tin before removing.

ENJOY.

NOTES AND INSPIRATION

Spoon batter into a loaf tin and bake for 1 hour for the most magnificent bread.

QUINOA, SPINACH AND FETA MUFFINS

These muffins make the perfect portable breakfast, lunch or snack. They're also delicious with chopped roasted vegetables such as pumpkin, capsicum or zucchini folded through the mixture, so experiment with whatever veg you have in the fridge.

GLUTEN-FREE | PROTEIN | ANTIOXIDANTS

INGREDIENTS

200 g baby spinach leaves

1 tablespoon extra-virgin olive oil

280 g (2 cups) cooked quinoa

4 large free-range eggs

60 g (¾ cup) grated parmesan

zest of 1 lemon

1 bunch parsley, chopped

pinch of sea salt and white pepper

90 g feta, chopped

2 tablespoons pine nuts

Makes 8 large or 6 regular muffins

PREHEAT your oven to 180°C fan-forced. Grease 6 large or 8 regular muffin tin holes.

SAUTÉ baby spinach in the olive oil on a gentle heat until lightly wilted.

COMBINE with the cooked quinoa, eggs, parmesan, lemon zest and parsley and season with salt and white pepper.

DIVIDE the mixture between the prepared muffin tin holes and top with feta and pine nuts.

BAKE for 25–30 minutes until cooked through.

ENJOY warm or cold.

NOTES AND INSPIRATION

These protein-rich muffins will keep in the fridge for up to 3 days.

GLUTEN-FREE BLUEBERRY SCONES

A wholesome gluten-free scone that's scented with olive oil, cinnamon and vanilla. I love serving these with a generous dollop of blueberry jam and coconut yoghurt.

GLUTEN-FREE | PLANT-BASED | DAIRY-FREE | GUT FRIENDLY

INGREDIENTS

240 g (2 cups) buckwheat flour

200 g (2 cups) almond meal, plus extra to sprinkle

1 tablespoon gluten-free baking powder

1 teaspoon cinnamon

125 ml (½ cup) extra-virgin olive oil

250 ml (1 cup) almond milk

60 ml (¼ cup) pure maple syrup

2 teaspoons vanilla extract

250 g frozen or fresh blueberries

Makes 16 scones

PREHEAT your oven to 160°C fan-forced. Line a baking tray with baking paper.

COMBINE buckwheat flour, almond meal, baking powder and cinnamon in a bowl.

MIX the olive oil, almond milk, maple syrup and vanilla together in a separate bowl then pour over the dry ingredients.

COMBINE into a soft sticky dough, adding a touch more almond milk if required.

FOLD in the blueberries.

SCOOP out the scone mix using an ice-cream scoop for even portioning onto the prepared tray.

SPRINKLE with almond meal.

BAKE for 30 minutes or until cooked through.

SERVE warm or at room temperature.

NOTES AND INSPIRATION

You can also make these scones in wedges – see Gluten-Free Scones on page 170 for instructions.

APPLE AND OLIVE OIL MUFFINS WITH CREAM CHEESE FROSTING

Olive oil is my favourite and I use it liberally in all types of cooking because it tastes beautiful and it's teeming with health benefits. It also makes these muffins so moist and delicious, you can't stop eating them.

PROTEIN | SUPERFOOD | LOW GI | HIGH FIBRE

INGREDIENTS

280 g (2¼ cups) wholemeal spelt flour

pinch of sea salt

½ teaspoon ground cinnamon

½ teaspoon baking powder

1 teaspoon bicarbonate of soda (baking soda)

125 ml (½ cup) light-flavoured extra-virgin olive oil

60 ml (¼ cup) honey

3 free-range eggs

1 teaspoon vanilla paste

100 g (⅔ cup) raisins or muscatels

zest and juice of 1 orange

2 large red apples, skin on, diced

1 quantity Lightened Up Cream Cheese Frosting (p 253)

Makes 12 scones

PREHEAT your oven to 160°C fan-forced. Lightly grease a 12-hole muffin tin or line with paper cases.

COMBINE flour, salt, cinnamon, baking powder and baking soda in a large bowl.

ADD olive oil, honey, eggs, vanilla, raisins and orange juice and zest and mix through until combined. Fold in the apple.

SPOON into the muffin tin. I like using my ice-cream scoop for this job, making it easy to portion equal amounts.

BAKE for 30–35 minutes or until firm to touch and cooked through.

REMOVE from the oven and cool.

SPREAD the frosting over muffins and enjoy.

NOTES AND INSPIRATION

Garnish muffins with roasted walnuts.

CARROT AND APPLE MUFFINS

This is carrot cake given the healthy breakfast makeover! These muffins are so yummy and moist and full of heart-protecting omega-3 fats, immune-boosting protein, as well as vitamin E to help promote healthy skin.

WELLBEING | GUT FRIENDLY | HIGH FIBRE

INGREDIENTS

- 250 g carrots, grated
- 250 g apples, skin on, grated or finely sliced
- 130 g (1 cup) raisins
- 60 ml (¼ cup) extra-virgin olive oil
- 1 teaspoon vanilla extract
- 80 ml (⅓ cup) raw honey
- 125 ml (½ cup) orange juice, freshly squeezed
- 3 free-range eggs
- 300 g (2½ cups) wholemeal spelt flour
- 2 teaspoons gluten-free baking powder
- 120 g (1¼ cups) walnuts

Topping

- 100 g (1 cup) rolled oats
- 60 g (½ cup) pumpkin seeds
- 30 g (¼ cup) sunflower seeds
- 50 g butter
- 2 teaspoons raw honey

Makes 12 muffins

PREHEAT your oven to 170°C fan-forced. Line a 12-hole muffin tin with paper cases.

COMBINE grated carrot, apple, raisins, olive oil, vanilla, honey, orange juice and eggs in a mixing bowl.

ADD the spelt flour, baking powder and walnuts.

MIX well with your hands until mixture is combined.

SPOON mixture into the muffin tin.

To make the topping:

COMBINE the oats and seeds in a mixing bowl.

RUB in the butter with your fingertips until evenly distributed throughout the mixture.

ADD honey and mix through lightly. The mix should be crumbly and delicious.

TOP the muffins with the crumble and bake for 30–40 minutes.

NOTES AND INSPIRATION

Use Greek yoghurt in place of orange juice.

YOGHURT BUCKWHEAT MUFFINS

This is a mood-boosting muffin to start your day. It's made with buckwheat flour, which is gluten-free and contains tryptophan, an amino acid that helps produce feel-good hormones in the body.

PROTEIN | GUT FRIENDLY | LOW GI | GLUTEN-FREE

INGREDIENTS

- 200 g red apples, skin on, finely chopped or sliced
- 60 ml (¼ cup) extra-virgin olive oil
- 2 tablespoons pure maple syrup or raw honey
- ½ teaspoon ground cinnamon
- 75 g (½ cup) raisins, soaked in water for 30 minutes
- 2 free-range eggs
- 125 ml (½ cup) rice milk
- 85 g (½ cup) brown rice flour
- 100 g (¾ cup) buckwheat flour
- 2 teaspoons gluten-free baking powder

Yoghurt Cream

- 250 ml (1 cup) strained cultured yoghurt (labneh)
- 2 tablespoons pure maple syrup
- 1 teaspoon vanilla paste

Makes 6 large muffins

PREHEAT your oven to 160°C fan-forced. Line 6 muffin tin holes with paper cases.

COMBINE apples, olive oil, maple syrup, cinnamon, raisins, eggs and rice milk in a large bowl.

ADD rice flour, buckwheat flour and baking powder. Mix until combined.

SPOON into the muffin tin cases.

BAKE for 35 minutes or until golden.

COOL muffins completely.

COMBINE strained yoghurt, maple syrup and vanilla to make the Yoghurt Cream.

FROST cupcakes with a dollop of the Yoghurt Cream.

NOTES AND INSPIRATION

For a dairy-free muffin, serve without the Yoghurt Cream. Garnish the muffins with fresh blueberries or chopped nuts.

PUMPKIN SCONES

Pumpkin is a great source of anti-inflammatory antioxidants that support a healthy immune system. It also contains potassium, which helps restore the body's balance of electrolytes.

VEGAN | DAIRY-FREE | NUT FREE | WHOLEFOOD

INGREDIENTS

240 g (2 cups) wholemeal spelt flour

1 teaspoon ground cinnamon

½ teaspoon sea salt

2 teaspoons gluten-free baking powder

250 g (1 cup) smashed roasted pumpkin

60 ml (¼ cup) extra-virgin olive oil

1 tablespoon raw honey or maple syrup

80 g (½ cup) raisins

100 g (1 cup) rolled oats

Makes 10 scones

PREHEAT your oven to 180°C fan-forced. Line a baking tray with baking paper.

COMBINE spelt flour, cinnamon, sea salt and baking powder in a bowl.

COMBINE smashed roasted pumpkin, olive oil and honey in another bowl, then add the raisins.

ADD pumpkin mix to the flour mix and combine gently with your fingertips.

TRANSFER dough onto a clean working surface covered with oats.

FLATTEN out the pumpkin scone dough to about 5 cm thick.

CUT the scones into rounds using a cutter or cut into wedges like the Gluten-Free Scones (see p 170).

PLACE the scones onto the prepared tray.

BAKE for 30 minutes until golden.

NOTES AND INSPIRATION

Enjoy topped with almond or macadamia butter.

GLUTEN-FREE SCONES

Here is a wonderful scone recipe bursting with goodness. They're simple to bake and extremely delicious to eat. The addition of natural kefir or buttermilk makes these scones light and fluffy, a fantastic result that's reminiscent of what true home cooking should be.

LOW GI | HIGH FIBRE | WELLBEING | GLUTEN-FREE

INGREDIENTS

280 g (2¼ cups) gluten-free flour, cup for cup

3 tablespoons tapioca starch or cornflour

3 teaspoons gluten-free baking powder

½ teaspoon sea salt flakes

120 g cold butter, grated

310 ml (1¼ cups) natural kefir or buttermilk, plus extra to brush

1 tablespoon raw honey

1 free-range egg

1 teaspoon vanilla extract

200 g fresh blueberries or 120 g (¾ cup) raisins

Makes 8 scones

PREHEAT your oven to 200°C fan-forced. Line a baking tray with baking paper.

COMBINE flour, tapioca starch or cornflour, baking powder and salt in a large bowl.

ADD the grated butter and rub through gently with your fingers.

COMBINE buttermilk, honey, egg and vanilla in a separate bowl.

ADD the buttermilk mixture to the flour.

MIX through gently until a sticky dough forms.

ADD blueberries or raisins and give the dough one more brief mix.

TURN out the dough onto a clean, lightly floured working surface.

SHAPE into a round 5 cm-thick disc and transfer onto the lined baking tray.

CUT into 8 triangular portions. Alternatively, you can scoop out 8 scones using an ice-cream scoop.

BRUSH the top with a little extra kefir or buttermilk.

BAKE for 20 minutes until cooked through.

NOTES AND INSPIRATION

Top with blueberry jam and Greek yoghurt and enjoy.

UGLY SCONES

The yoghurt in this recipe makes this dough light with a subtle sourdough flavour that marries perfectly with good strawberry jam. Enjoy them on a Sunday morning accompanied by freshly brewed black filter coffee.

GUT FRIENDLY | ENERGISING | ALL NATURAL

INGREDIENTS

280 g (2¼ cups) spelt flour

3 teaspoons baking powder

½ teaspoon sea salt

300 g (1 cup) Greek yoghurt

125 ml (½ cup) milk, any kind

1 tablespoon raw honey

Makes 8 scones

PREHEAT your oven to 180°C fan-forced. Line a baking tray with baking paper.

COMBINE spelt flour, baking powder and salt in a bowl.

IN a separate bowl, combine the yoghurt, milk and honey.

POUR the yoghurt mixture into the flour.

MIX lightly with a fork or knife until you achieve a soft, sticky dough.

SCOOP out 8 portions onto the prepared baking tray using an ice-cream scoop, or just dollop with a spoon or your hands.

BAKE for 15 minutes until golden.

SERVE warm with jam and yoghurt.

NOTES AND INSPIRATION

Scoop out portions onto a heated non-stick pan and cook over a gentle heat with the lid on for 3–4 minutes each side until golden. Add raisins or blueberries, or for a savoury scone, omit the honey and add chopped chives, grated zucchini and a handful of cheddar.

SPELT AND HONEY SCONES

I love using wholemeal spelt flour in this recipe as it gives a divine crumb and delightful wholesome flavour when you bite into it. The rolled oats add another layer of texture and goodness and are perfect married with the honey, cinnamon and vanilla.

HIGH FIBRE | WHOLEFOOD | GUT FRIENDLY

INGREDIENTS

240 g (2 cups) wholemeal spelt flour

3 teaspoons baking powder

½ teaspoon ground cinnamon

100 g butter

1 teaspoon vanilla paste

1 tablespoon raw honey or maple syrup

125 ml (½ cup) milk (any kind), plus extra to brush

100 g fresh dates, pitted and cut into chunks

100 g (1 cup) rolled oats

Makes 12 scones

PREHEAT your oven to 180°C fan-forced. Line a baking tray with baking paper.

COMBINE spelt flour, baking powder and cinnamon.

RUB in the butter gently using your fingertips or a food processor.

COMBINE vanilla, honey and milk in a separate bowl, then pour into the dry ingredients.

ADD the dates.

MIX lightly to form a soft dough.

SPRINKLE with oats so that it coats the entire scone dough.

FLATTEN the dough on a work surface lightly dusted with spelt flour if needed.

CUT into rounds and place on the prepared baking tray.

BRUSH tops with a little extra milk.

BAKE for 20–25 minutes until golden.

SERVE warm or at room temperature and enjoy.

NOTES AND INSPIRATION

Serve with Strawberry and Vanilla Jam (p 249).

CHOCOLATE RASPBERRY MUFFINS

What I love about making these muffins is that they are a one-bowl muffin mix that takes about 5 minutes to bring together. All you need to do is to pop them into the oven for the magic to happen.

DAIRY-FREE | GRAIN-FREE | GLUTEN-FREE | NUT-FREE

INGREDIENTS

6 free-range eggs

1 teaspoon vanilla extract

2 tablespoons raw honey

60 ml (¼ cup) extra-virgin olive oil or coconut oil

70 g (½ cup) coconut flour

2 teaspoons gluten-free baking powder

80 g (½ cup) raspberries

60 g good-quality 85% dark eating chocolate, chopped

melted chocolate and raspberries, to serve (optional)

Makes 6–10 muffins

PREHEAT your oven to 160°C fan-forced.

LINE a muffin tin with paper cases. You should get approximately 10 small muffins or 6 large muffins from this mix.

MIX the eggs, vanilla and honey with a hand whisk in a large bowl.

POUR in the olive or coconut oil and mix well.

ADD the coconut flour and baking powder and mix until combined.

FOLD in raspberries and dark chocolate.

SPOON mixture into the muffin cases.

BAKE for 35–40 minutes or until cooked through.

COOL for at least 30 minutes.

DECORATE with melted chocolate and raspberries if you like.

NOTES AND INSPIRATION

These delicious muffins will keep covered in the fridge for up to 4 days. Swap raspberries for cherries.

BISCUITS + COOKIES

VEGAN CHOC-CHIP COOKIES

This is the world's healthiest chocolate-chip cookie recipe! They're super easy to make and the secret is to use good-quality dark chocolate, which makes them so irresistible. I always double or triple the recipe when I make these because they don't last long.

PROTEIN | VEGAN | GLUTEN-FREE

INGREDIENTS

300 g (3 cups) almond meal

100 ml cold-pressed macadamia nut oil or coconut oil

100 ml pure maple syrup

1 teaspoon vanilla extract

100 g dark chocolate chips or chopped pieces

slivered almonds, to garnish

Makes 12 cookies

PREHEAT your oven to a low 130°C fan-forced. Line a baking tray with baking paper.

COMBINE almond meal, oil, maple syrup and vanilla in a bowl.

MIX and form into a dough. Add a splash of water (1–2 teaspoons) to help form a dough if needed.

ADD chocolate pieces and mix in.

USING a small ice-cream scoop, form dough into 12 cookies. Place them on the prepared baking tray.

PRESS down on each cookie lightly with a fork and top each cookie with a slivered almond.

BAKE for 30 minutes until golden.

COOL completely before devouring!

NOTES AND INSPIRATION

Add 2 tablespoons raw cacao to create double choc-chip cookies.

OATMEAL CHOC-CHIP COOKIES

The secret to making these chocolate-chip cookies lies in the mixing. Make sure the ingredients are gently combined so that the oats remain intact.

ANTIOXIDANTS | HIGH FIBRE | WELLBEING

INGREDIENTS

200 g (2 cups) rolled oats

50 g (½ cup) desiccated coconut

60 ml (¼ cup) extra-virgin olive oil or macadamia oil

60 ml (¼ cup) pure maple syrup or raw honey

1 free-range egg

100 g good-quality 70% dark eating chocolate

Makes 12 cookies

PREHEAT your oven to 150°C fan-forced. Line a baking tray with baking paper.

COMBINE oats, coconut, olive or macadamia oil, maple syrup and egg in a mixing bowl.

MIX through with your hands for a few minutes, massaging the ingredients until the cookie dough starts to come together. Alternatively, you can mix with a stand mixer.

REST the mixture for 5 minutes so the oats soften a little more and hold together.

CHOP the chocolate into small pieces with a large knife and mix through the cookie dough.

SCOOP small, delicate portions of cookie dough mixture using an ice-cream scoop or a spoon onto the baking tray and flatten slightly.

BAKE for 20 minutes or until golden.

REMOVE from the oven to cool completely and enjoy.

NOTES AND INSPIRATION

Carob can be used in place of dark chocolate.

GRAHAM CRACKER BISCUITS

These delicious biscuits are also known as granita or digestive biscuits. They are wholesome, low in refined sugar and high in fibre, which helps support digestion.

HIGH FIBRE | GUT FRIENDLY | LOW GI

INGREDIENTS

130 g (1 cup) oat flour or oat bran

150 g (1¼ cup) wholemeal spelt flour

60 g (¼ cup) coconut sugar or unrefined raw sugar

1 teaspoon gluten-free baking powder

½ teaspoon sea salt

150 g cold butter, cut into cubes

60 ml (¼ cup) cold water

1 teaspoon vanilla extract

Egg Wash

1 free-range egg

2 tablespoons milk

Makes 18–24 biscuits

PREHEAT your oven to 160° C fan-forced. Line a baking tray with baking paper.

COMBINE oat flour, spelt flour, sugar, baking powder and sea salt in a mixing bowl.

ADD butter, rubbing it into the flour mixture until it resembles coarse breadcrumbs. You can do this by hand or use a food processor.

COMBINE water and vanilla then pour into the biscuit crumb mixture.

MIX well until you get a soft dough.

DUST the dough with a little oat flour then turn out onto a clean work surface.

FLATTEN out the dough slightly then wrap in cling film and rest in the fridge for 30 minutes to 1 hour.

REMOVE from the fridge and roll out the dough using a rolling pin. Dust the dough with a little oat flour to prevent any sticking. The dough should be about 5 mm thick.

CUT the dough into rounds using a cookie cutter and arrange on the prepared baking tray.

PRICK the dough with a fork and brush with the combined egg wash ingredients.

BAKE for 30 minutes or until golden.

COOL completely and enjoy.

NOTES AND INSPIRATION

Serve with a pot of your favourite tea.

PEANUT BUTTER COOKIES

Peanut butter is deliciously addictive! I can eat it straight out of a jar—it's just pure comfort food that satisfies me for hours. What I love about these cookies is that you only need a few ingredients to create pure magic.

DAIRY-FREE | GRAIN-FREE | PALEO | PROTEIN

INGREDIENTS

250 g (1 cup) natural peanut butter

2 tablespoons raw honey or pure maple syrup

1 free-range egg

1 teaspoon vanilla paste

70 g (½ cup) peanuts, roughly chopped

pinch of sea salt flakes

Makes 12 cookies

PREHEAT your oven to 160°C fan-forced. Line a baking tray with baking paper.

COMBINE peanut butter, honey, egg and vanilla in a mixing bowl.

MIX well until combined. The mixture will be soft and slightly sticky.

SPOON delicate portions onto the baking tray using an ice-cream scoop or a spoon.

GARNISH with peanuts.

PRESS the cookie down so it flattens.

SPRINKLE lightly with a little flaked sea salt.

BAKE for 30 minutes or until golden.

REMOVE from oven to cool and enjoy.

NOTES AND INSPIRATION

Use cashew butter or almond butter in place of peanut butter for variation. For a crunchier cookie, you can add a few tablespoons of almond meal or desiccated coconut.

SALTED BUCKWHEAT COOKIES

It's hard to believe that these salted chocolate cookies are brimming with antioxidants, fibre and healthy fats. This is one scrumptious cookie to enjoy with a steaming mug of hot chocolate or a chai tea.

GLUTEN-FREE | HIGH FIBRE | WELLBEING

INGREDIENTS

240 g (1 cup) butter

80 g (½ cup) coconut sugar, rapadura or raw sugar

1 teaspoon vanilla extract

1 teaspoon sea salt

1 teaspoon ground cinnamon

240 g (2 cups) buckwheat flour

60 g (½ cup) cacao powder

½ teaspoon gluten-free baking powder

2 teaspoons cold-pressed coffee or chilled espresso

pinch of sea salt flakes, to garnish

Makes 24 cookies

PREHEAT your oven to 160°C fan-forced. Line 1–2 baking trays with baking paper.

COMBINE butter, sugar, vanilla, salt and cinnamon in the mixing bowl of a stand mixer.

BEAT for 8 minutes until fluffy and creamy.

COMBINE buckwheat flour, cacao powder and baking powder in a separate bowl.

ADD dry ingredients to the creamed butter, along with the coffee.

MIX well using the paddle attachment until combined.

SPOON cookie mix onto the baking trays using an ice-cream scoop or a spoon.

FLATTEN down slightly and garnish with sea salt flakes.

BAKE for 30 minutes then remove from the oven to cool completely.

NOTES AND INSPIRATION

Add 100 g finely chopped good-quality 70% dark eating chocolate for double chocolate-chip cookies.

TAHINI AND HEMP COOKIES

These cookies are a nourishing treat, packed with heart-healthy fats and protein. Made with almond meal and sweetened naturally with maple syrup, they offer a gluten-free, protein-rich snack that satisfies cravings while fuelling your body with wholesome goodness.

GLUTEN-FREE | GUT FRIENDLY | PROTEIN

INGREDIENTS

125 ml (½ cup) tahini

60 ml (¼ cup) pure maple syrup or raw honey

2 teaspoons vanilla extract

pinch of sea salt

½ teaspoon baking powder

100 g (1 cup) almond meal

hemp seeds or sesame seeds, for rolling

Makes 10 cookies

PREHEAT your oven to 160°C fan-forced. Line a baking tray with baking paper.

COMBINE tahini, maple syrup and vanilla in a mixing bowl.

ADD the salt, baking powder and almond meal and mix into a soft dough.

DIVIDE into 10 biscuits using an ice-cream scoop for easy measuring.

ROLL each biscuit in hemp or sesame seeds and place on the baking tray.

GENTLY press each cookie with your hands or the base of a glass.

BAKE for 20 minutes until cooked through.

COOL completely and enjoy.

NOTES AND INSPIRATION

Add the zest from 1 orange. Cookies will store for up to 1 week.

OLIVE OIL ANZAC BISCUITS

Using wholemeal spelt flour and extra-virgin olive oil in this recipe gives the biscuits a wonderful flavour and offers a healthy twist on a traditional treat.

HEART HEALTHY | HIGH FIBRE | ALL NATURAL

INGREDIENTS

175 g (1¾ cups) rolled oats

150 g (1½ cups) desiccated coconut

150 g (1¼ cups) wholemeal spelt flour

½ teaspoon bicarbonate of soda (baking soda)

125 ml (½ cup) extra-virgin olive oil

125 ml (½ cup) pure maple syrup

60 ml (¼ cup) hot water

Makes 18 biscuits

PREHEAT your oven to 160°C fan-forced. Line 1–2 baking trays with baking paper.

COMBINE oats, coconut, spelt flour and baking soda in a mixing bowl.

ADD olive oil, maple syrup and hot water then mix well.

PLACE spoonfuls of dough on baking trays.

FLATTEN down with your fingertips.

BAKE for 20 minutes until golden.

COOL and enjoy.

NOTES AND INSPIRATION

Dunk into icy cold milk before devouring.

HONEY AND VANILLA MADELEINES

I used to make stacks of these delicate treats when I was the pastry chef in a hotel in Western Australia. These little morsels are delicious dunked into your morning coffee or used for a celebration trifle or tiramisu.

GLUTEN-FREE | HEART HEALTHY | ALL NATURAL

INGREDIENTS

3 large free-range eggs

zest of 1 orange

80 ml (⅓ cup) raw honey

1 teaspoon vanilla extract

125 ml (½ cup) extra-virgin olive oil or melted butter

40 g (½ cup) almond meal

90 g (⅔ cup) rice flour

3 tablespoons tapioca flour

½ teaspoon gluten-free baking powder

pinch of sea salt

icing sugar, to serve

Makes 12 madeleines

BEAT eggs, orange zest, honey and vanilla for 6 minutes until light and fluffy.

POUR in the olive oil or butter, then add the almond meal, rice flour, tapioca flour, baking powder and salt. Mix well.

REST in the fridge for 30 minutes.

PREHEAT your oven to 160°C fan-forced. Lightly oil a madeleine tin.

PIPE or spoon the madeleine batter into the madeleine moulds.

BAKE for 10–12 minutes until golden and cooked through.

REMOVE from the oven and flip out onto a cooling rack.

SERVE dusted with a little icing sugar

NOTES AND INSPIRATION

You could also serve the madeleines with thick Greek yoghurt and apricot preserves or a drizzle of honey. Use as a gluten-free alternative for savoiardi biscuits for your next tiramisu.

RAW MAUI COOKIES

These raw cookies are loaded with the protein, fibre and minerals your body craves. They only take a couple of minutes to make and can be enjoyed as a quick healthy snack any time of day.

PALEO | PROTEIN | DAIRY-FREE

INGREDIENTS

200 g natural peanut or almond butter

150 g fresh dates, pitted

250 g (2½ cups) rolled oats

50 g (½ cup) desiccated coconut

pinch of sea salt

pinch of cinnamon

1 teaspoon vanilla paste

35 g (¼ cup) pumpkin seeds

Makes 16 cookies

COMBINE peanut butter, dates, oats, coconut, sea salt, cinnamon and vanilla in a food processor.

MIX until combined and the mixture resembles breadcrumbs.

ADD 1–2 tablespoons of water and mix again so that the mixture sticks together when pressed.

FORM into cookies using a small ice-cream scoop or spoon and place on a plate or baking tray.

GARNISH with pumpkin seeds.

SET in the fridge for at least 1 hour before eating.

STORE in the fridge for up to 1 week.

NOTES AND INSPIRATION

For a little variety replace the peanut butter with macadamia butter.

BANANA OATMEAL COOKIES

This is a power-packed cookie that will energise and sustain your body for hours! They're so simple to make and are the perfect lunchbox addition.

WELLBEING | LOW GI | HIGH FIBRE

INGREDIENTS

150 g (½ cup) mashed ripe banana

½ teaspoon ground cinnamon

200 g (2 cups) rolled oats

50 g (½ cup) desiccated coconut

75 g (½ cup) raisins

60 ml (¼ cup) pure maple syrup

60 ml (¼ cup) extra-virgin olive oil or soft butter

Makes 12 cookies

PREHEAT your oven to 130°C fan-forced. Line a baking tray with baking paper.

COMBINE all the ingredients in a large mixing bowl.

MIX together well with your hands, squeezing the mixture until it starts to bind. To make it easier, you can also use a food processor.

FORM into 12 cookies using a small ice-cream scoop to equally portion out the mixture. Place on the prepared tray.

FLATTEN the cookies slightly with a fork.

BAKE for 35 minutes or until golden.

COOL and enjoy.

NOTES AND INSPIRATION

Add chocolate chips in place of raisins.

CHOC-CHIP OLIVE OIL COOKIES

These chocolate-chip cookies are made with heart-healthy extra-virgin olive oil, omega-3 rich walnuts and quality dark chocolate—the perfect treat for when you're craving a little sweet goodness.

ALL NATURAL | ENERGISING | HEART HEALTHY

INGREDIENTS

125 ml (½ cup) extra-virgin olive oil

2 large free-range eggs

3 tablespoons pure maple syrup

2 teaspoons vanilla extract

pinch of sea salt

60 g (¼ cup) coconut sugar

240 g (2 cups) gluten-free flour or wholemeal spelt flour

60 g (½ cup) almond meal

1 generous teaspoon baking powder

100 g good-quality 70% dark eating chocolate, chopped

100 g (1 cup) walnuts, chopped

Makes 12 cookies

PREHEAT your oven to 160°C fan-forced. Line a baking tray with baking paper.

COMBINE olive oil, eggs, maple syrup, vanilla, salt and coconut sugar in a bowl and whisk until combined.

ADD the flour, almond meal and baking powder and mix with a spoon to form a soft dough.

MIX through the chocolate and walnuts, making sure they are evenly distributed throughout the dough.

SCOOP out 12 portions of cookie dough onto the prepared baking tray and flatten with wet hands.

BAKE for 20–25 minutes.

COOL before devouring.

NOTES AND INSPIRATION

Make a double batch—these will disappear quickly!

VANILLA TEA BISCUITS

Reminiscent of a classic Monte Carlo, these buttery shortbreads are ever so light and they melt in the mouth. You can also enjoy them sandwiched together with raspberry jam and a dollop of cream cheese or mascarpone.

ALL NATURAL | ENERGISING | STRESS RELIEF

INGREDIENTS

150 g slightly salted butter, softened

2 teaspoons vanilla extract

60 g (⅓ cup) icing sugar

200 g (1¾ cups) spelt flour

60 g (⅓ cup) cornflour

2 teaspoons baking powder

Makes 12 biscuits

PREHEAT your oven to 160°C fan-forced. Line a baking tray with baking paper.

COMBINE the butter, vanilla and icing sugar in a food processor along with the spelt flour, cornflour and baking powder.

PULSE the mixture for a few seconds, until the butter is rubbed into the flour.

ADD 1 tablespoon of water and form into a soft dough.

REFRIGERATE the dough for 30 minutes.

ROLL the dough between two sheets of baking paper. Cut into circles using a biscuit cutter and arrange on the prepared baking tray. Decorate biscuits by spiking with a fork.

BAKE for 15–20 minutes or until slightly golden.

COOL on the tray and store in an airtight container for up to 2 weeks.

NOTES AND INSPIRATION

Sandwich biscuits with a creamy gelato for a spectacular ice-cream sandwich.

SAVOURY BAKES

KALE, SPINACH AND FETA PIE

This is a delicious meal that I often make for my weekday dinner or as a portable healthy lunch. Preparation is effortless and the final result is beautiful—the fresh subtle flavours of green dance in your mouth.

SUPERFOOD | GLUTEN-FREE | PROTEIN

INGREDIENTS

2 leeks, washed and finely sliced

1 tablespoon olive oil

1 bunch kale or cavolo nero, washed, trimmed and finely shredded

200 g baby spinach leaves

generous pinch of black pepper

zest of 1 lemon

1 bunch parsley, chopped

6 free-range eggs

80 g feta, crumbled

small handful of pine nuts

Serves 4

PREHEAT oven to 180°C fan-forced. Lightly grease a 22 cm pie dish or line with baking paper.

SAUTÉ leeks in olive oil in a large heavy-based pan until softened.

ADD kale and cook for 5 minutes until soft and wilted.

ADD baby spinach leaves. You may need to add this in two lots and cook through until just wilted.

SEASON with black pepper and add lemon zest and parsley.

SPOON the kale and spinach mixture into the pie dish.

BREAK eggs into a bowl and whisk lightly until combined.

POUR the eggs over the greens and gently incorporate through the mix of green goodness.

SPRINKLE the feta and pine nuts over the top.

BAKE for 40–45 minutes or until firm to touch and golden.

REMOVE from the oven and rest for 5 minutes before serving.

NOTES AND INSPIRATION

Use ricotta in place of feta. Serve with a large garden salad made simply of leaves drizzled with French-style dressing.

SPINACH, RICOTTA AND SWEET POTATO TART

Packed with protein to sustain lean muscle and calcium for good bone health, ricotta is satiating and nourishing for the body and gives this tart a divinely soft and creamy texture. The addition of sweet potatoes and leafy greens provides B vitamins and antioxidants.

VEGETARIAN | LOW GI | PROTEIN | GUT FRIENDLY

INGREDIENTS

1 kg firm ricotta, drained

6 free-range eggs

750 g blanched or frozen chopped spinach, moisture squeezed out

1 bunch parsley, chopped

sea salt, to taste

1 large sweet potato, shaved into fine ribbons

2 tablespoons extra-virgin olive oil

Serves 8

PREHEAT your oven to 160°C fan-forced. Line a 25 cm round baking tin with baking paper.

COMBINE ricotta and eggs in a mixing bowl.

ADD the spinach, parsley and a generous pinch of salt and mix until combined, then pour into the baking tin.

TOSS sweet potato ribbons with the olive oil and cover the top of the tart loosely. It will seem like a lot but the sweet potato will collapse as it cooks.

BAKE for 60–75 minutes or until set. The top of the tart should wobble when touched when it's ready.

REMOVE from the oven and allow to come to room temperature before removing from the tin.

SERVE and enjoy.

NOTES AND INSPIRATION

Use blanched silverbeet (chard) in place of spinach. Serve warm or cold with leafy greens. Decorate with crispy fried sage leaves if desired.

CAULIFLOWER LEEK MAC AND CHEESE

My veggie twist on a classic mac and cheese that's brimming with health and goodness. Leeks and steamed cauliflower provide wonderful myriad antioxidants and prebiotic fibre for digestive health as well as forming an aromatic base for freshly cooked pasta.

WELLBEING | ENERGISING | STRESS RELIEF

INGREDIENTS

2 large leeks, halved lengthways and thinly sliced

2 tablespoons extra-virgin olive oil

500 ml (2 cups) hot water from the kettle

1 cauliflower, cut into florets

250 g short pasta (I used gluten-free)

250 g ricotta

60 g (¾ cup) grated parmesan

handful parsley, chopped

sea salt and white pepper, to taste

handful of breadcrumbs (optional)

Serves 4

SAUTÉ the leeks in the olive oil in a large, heavy-based, ovenproof pan over a low to medium heat for 10 minutes until softened but not coloured.

POUR over the water and simmer for 20–30 minutes until the leeks are silky and creamy.

MEANWHILE, steam the cauliflower florets for 8 minutes until tender.

PREHEAT your oven to 200°C fan-forced.

BOIL the pasta in plenty of salted boiling water until al dente, then strain, reserving 1 cup of the cooking water.

ADD the ricotta to the leeks and mix in half of the pasta cooking water to form a sauce.

FOLD through the cauliflower, pasta, parmesan, parsley and more water if needed. Season with salt and white pepper.

SPRINKLE with breadcrumbs if using. Place pan in the oven and bake for 15 minutes until golden.

SERVE immediately and enjoy.

NOTES AND INSPIRATION

Swap the cauliflower for broccoli for a colourful alternative.

BAKED RICOTTA DUMPLINGS IN TOMATO

This is a simple way of making ricotta dumplings without boiling them in water. It's also high in protein and loaded with flavour.

LOW GI | ENERGISING | STRESS RELIEF

INGREDIENTS

200 g spinach, blanched, squeezed and chopped

500 g firm ricotta, strained

60 g (¾ cup) grated parmesan, plus extra to sprinkle

1 large free-range egg

sea salt, to taste

100 g (⅔ cup) rice flour, spelt flour or gluten-free flour, plus extra for dusting

750 ml (3 cups) passata

Embellishments

Aged balsamic vinegar, salad leaves, basil, pine nuts

Serves 6

PREHEAT your oven to 180°C fan-forced.

COMBINE the spinach, ricotta, parmesan and egg in a large bowl. Mix well until combined and season with a pinch of salt.

MIX in flour until combined.

MAKE the dumplings by shaping the mix into bite-sized balls and placing them onto a lightly floured baking tray. A small ice-cream scoop is great for this.

POUR the passata into a baking dish or pan. The sauce needs to come at least halfway up the side of the dumplings so be generous.

ARRANGE the dumplings in the tomato sauce and sprinkle with extra parmesan.

BAKE for 25–30 minutes or until the dumplings are hot and the sauce is bubbling.

SERVE straight from the pan with fresh basil and your choice of embellishments.

NOTES AND INSPIRATION

You can replace spinach with silverbeet or cavolo nero.

VEGETABLE LASAGNE

One of my favourite meals is a nourishing vegetable lasagne. I often make a large tray of it over the weekend then cut it into portions and freeze them, so I can easily have a meal on the table anytime I want—especially when pressed for time during the week. It's also a great dish for impromptu dinner parties and a tasty portable meal that everyone can enjoy.

GLUTEN-FREE | PROTEIN | SUPERFOOD | WELLBEING

INGREDIENTS

Smashed Tomato Sauce

3 French shallots, finely diced

2 tablespoons olive oil

1.2 kg ripe Roma tomatoes, chopped

pinch of sea salt

1 tablespoon butter

Lasagne

1 kg zucchini

1 kg eggplant

olive oil, to brush

sea salt

1 kg sweet potato

sprinkle of ground cinnamon

4 red capsicums

¼ cup pesto

100 g baby spinach leaves

500 g firm deli-style ricotta

30 g parmesan cheese, finely grated

Serves 8–10

To make the Smashed Tomato Sauce:

SAUTÉ shallots in the olive oil in a saucepan over a medium heat for 1–2 minutes until soft.

ADD tomatoes and mix through.

COVER with a lid, reduce the heat slightly and leave to simmer for 10 minutes or until the tomatoes have softened and started to collapse.

REMOVE the lid and smash tomatoes with the back of a fork and season with salt.

WHISK in butter just before using.

To make the lasagne:

PREHEAT oven to 180°C fan-forced. Line 2–3 baking trays with baking paper.

SLICE zucchini into ribbons using a mandoline then place in a single layer on the baking tray.

ROAST for 10 minutes, or until the zucchini has lightly softened, then remove and set aside.

SLICE eggplant into 5 mm-thick pieces lengthways.

PLACE onto a baking tray in a single layer and lightly brush with olive oil. Season with a little salt.

ROAST in the oven for 30 minutes or until golden and soft. Remove and set aside.

THINLY slice sweet potato (with the skin) lengthways on a mandoline to form delicate orange wafers.

SAVOURY BAKES

LAY on a baking tray and lightly brush with olive oil.

SPRINKLE very lightly with a little cinnamon and salt and roast for 30 minutes or until softened. Remove and set aside.

HALVE the capsicums and remove their inner core.

LAY skin-side up on a baking tray and roast in the oven for 20–30 minutes or until softened and golden.

REMOVE capsicums from the tray. After 30 minutes, remove the skins from the capsicums and set aside.

To assemble lasagne:

SPOON 1 cup of the Smashed Tomato Sauce over the base of a large baking dish.

LAY a third of the roasted sweet potato over the base.

TOP with half the zucchini, spread 2 tablespoons of pesto on top and then a few handfuls of baby spinach.

LAY half of the eggplant on top and spread one cup of Smashed Tomato Sauce over that.

LAY all the roasted capsicum over this.

REPEAT the layering process from sweet potato to eggplant.

FINISH off with a layer of Smashed Tomato Sauce and sweet potato on the final layer.

BLEND the ricotta until smooth. Add ¼ cup of water if needed to form a smooth and creamy white sauce.

SPREAD sauce over the top of the lasagne and lightly sprinkle with parmesan.

BAKE for 40–45 minutes at 180°C or until golden and hot.

SERVE with a leafy green salad and more Smashed Tomato Sauce if desired.

NOTES AND INSPIRATION

Use store-bought passata if you don't have time to make the Smashed Tomato Sauce. The Polish make their lasagne using delicate, thin homemade crepes in place of pasta—it's how my great aunt used to make hers. If you like, add Spelt Crepes (p 246) to the layers alongside the roasted vegetables.

GENIUS 15-MINUTE PIZZA

A quick and easy pizza recipe that you can cook in around 15 minutes. The result will be a purely delicious pizza dough, which you can embellish with tomatoes, mozzarella and fresh basil.

ALL NATURAL | ENERGISING | VEGETARIAN

INGREDIENTS

200 g (1¾ cups) spelt flour

2 teaspoons baking powder

pinch of sea salt

125 ml (½ cup) warm water

1 tablespoon extra-virgin olive oil

1 tablespoon pure maple syrup or raw honey

semolina or rice flour, for dusting

Topping

3 generous tablespoons passata

1 tablespoon grated parmesan

1 ball buffalo mozzarella

extra-virgin olive oil, to drizzle

6 basil leaves, to garnish

Makes 1 large pizza

PREHEAT your oven to 250°C fan-forced.

COMBINE spelt flour, baking powder and salt in a mixing bowl.

POUR in the warm water, olive oil and maple syrup and start mixing immediately until combined and you have a soft, sticky dough. Dust with a little extra flour if required.

ROLL and stretch the dough into a round circle about the size of the frying pan you will use to cook your pizza. Sprinkle the base of your frying pan with a little semolina or rice flour to prevent any sticking.

CAREFULLY place the dough in the frying pan.

SPREAD a spoonful or two of passata over the top of the dough followed by a little grated parmesan.

ARRANGE over fresh mozzarella then caress the top with a little drizzle of olive oil.

COOK the pizza on the stove over medium heat for 3 minutes or until the bottom is golden and the top starts to puff up.

PLACE the pan in the oven and cook for another 6–8 minutes or until the cheese has melted and the top is crisp and golden brown.

SERVE IMMEDIATELY garnished with fresh basil.

NOTES AND INSPIRATION

Add your favourite toppings—olives, sliced mushroom and roasted capsicum are great.

SAVOURY BAKES

QUICK AND EASY QUICHE

This is a great quiche to whip up when you're short of time. Fill it with any leftover cooked vegetables you have lying around the fridge.

GLUTEN-FREE | GUT FRIENDLY | HIGH PROTEIN

INGREDIENTS

2 leeks, sliced

2 tablespoons extra-virgin olive oil

100 g baby spinach

pinch of sea salt and white pepper

6 large free-range eggs, beaten

2 tablespoons grated parmesan (optional)

300 g organic silken tofu or ricotta, drained

Serves 2–4

PREHEAT your oven to 200°C fan-forced. Line an ovenproof dish with baking paper.

COOK the leeks in the olive oil over a gentle heat until softened, but not coloured.

ADD the spinach and season with salt and white pepper. Cook until wilted, then place into a large bowl along with the beaten eggs and parmesan.

POUR the mixture into the prepared dish.

BREAK up the tofu or ricotta and place in the egg mixture.

BAKE for 20 minutes until golden and set.

REMOVE from the oven and serve hot or at room temperature.

NOTES AND INSPIRATION

I also love adding sweet potato chunks and serving with tomato relish and leafy greens. This quiche will keep in the fridge for up to 3 days.

ZUCCHINI AND RICOTTA TART

A classic spring and summer savoury tart that's perfect for a lunch with the girls or to take to a picnic with friends. Serve with a side salad made with baby gem or cos lettuce caressed with French-style vinaigrette.

WELLBEING | ENERGISING | ALL NATURAL

INGREDIENTS

650 g zucchini, thinly sliced

1 teaspoon sea salt

1 quantity Foolproof Pastry (p 237)

250 g firm ricotta

100 g Danish feta

2 tablespoons chopped chives

zest of 1 lemon

1 tablespoon extra-virgin olive oil

milk, to brush

leafy greens, to serve

Serves 4–6

PREHEAT your oven to 200°C fan-forced.

TOSS zucchini and salt in a bowl, then place in a colander for 15 minutes to allow any excess moisture to drain out.

PLACE the pastry on a sheet of baking paper and roll out until about 30 cm diameter. Transfer pastry and baking paper onto a baking tray. Refrigerate before using.

SMASH ricotta and feta in a bowl, then mix through the chives and lemon zest.

SPREAD the ricotta mixture on the pastry, leaving a 3 cm border around the edges.

ARRANGE the zucchini on top of the ricotta and brush with olive oil.

FOLD over the pastry to enclose the filling and brush with a little milk to glaze.

BAKE the tart for 40–45 minutes or until golden.

SERVE and enjoy with leafy greens tossed in a good vinaigrette.

NOTES AND INSPIRATION

Top with rocket leaves lightly coated with lemon juice and olive oil before serving.

ROAST PUMPKIN GALETTE

I absolutely love this French-style tart and often make it as a weekend dinner to enjoy with hubby. Pumpkin is high in antioxidants and fibre and the saltiness of the creamy feta complements it perfectly.

STRESS RELIEF | ENERGISING | ALL NATURAL

INGREDIENTS

1 kg pumpkin, peeled, seeds removed and chopped

extra-virgin olive oil, for cooking

sea salt, to taste

2 brown onions, thinly sliced

2 tablespoons good-quality aged balsamic vinegar

1 quantity Foolproof Pastry (p 237) or Simple Olive Oil Pastry (p 238)

100 g feta, any kind, to serve

handful chopped parsley or basil leaves, to serve

Embellishments

seeds of 1 pomegranate

30 g (⅓ cup) roasted walnuts or pistachio nuts

aged balsamic vinegar

Serves 4–6

PREHEAT your oven to 200°C fan-forced.

ARRANGE pumpkin on a baking tray and drizzle with a little olive oil. Add a pinch of sea salt. Roast the pumpkin for 30 minutes until soft.

SAUTÉ the onion with a little olive oil over a medium heat until softened. Remove from the heat and mix through the balsamic vinegar. Set aside.

PLACE the pastry between 2 large sheets of baking paper and roll out until about 40 cm in diameter, lightly dusting with a little flour to prevent sticking.

TRANSFER the pastry to a baking tray.

SPREAD over the caramelised onions, leaving a 3 cm border around the outside of the pastry dough.

SMASH the pumpkin roughly—you should have about 500 g of cooked pumpkin—then place over the onions.

FOLD in the pastry edges and brush with a little milk or water.

BAKE for 40–45 minutes until golden.

REMOVE from the oven and serve topped with feta and herbs.

EMBELLISH with pomegranate, nuts and a drizzle of aged balsamic vinegar.

NOTES AND INSPIRATION

Serve with steamed beans or leafy greens, lemon wedges and extra goat or Persian feta on the side.

VEGAN SPINACH TART WITH TOFU RICOTTA

This nourishing tart is high in fibre, heart-healthy fats and plant-based protein. The leek and spinach provide a boost of antioxidants and prebiotics to support digestive health, while olive oil offers anti-inflammatory benefits and nourishes skin. Silken tofu adds protein and calcium to support bone and muscle health.

WELLBEING | PROTEIN | PLANT-BASED

INGREDIENTS

1 quantity Foolproof Pastry (p 237) or Simple Olive Oil Pastry (p 238)

1 leek, halved and sliced

2 tablespoons extra-virgin olive oil

500 g silken tofu, drained

sea salt and white pepper, to taste

40 g (¼ cup) tapioca flour or cornflour

2 tablespoons nutritional yeast flakes (optional)

½ teaspoon turmeric powder

90 g (½ cup) pine nuts

400 g spinach, blanched, strained and chopped

handful parsley or basil leaves, lightly chopped

Serves 4

PREHEAT the oven to 180°C fan-forced.

ROLL out the pastry between 2 sheets of baking paper to about 30 cm diameter and set aside.

SAUTÉ the leek in the olive oil over a medium heat for 5–8 minutes until softened. Set aside to cool.

COMBINE the tofu, salt, pepper, tapioca flour, nutritional yeast, turmeric and pine nuts in a food processor. Blend until smooth and creamy.

FOLD in the leek, spinach and parsley and mix through lightly by hand.

LINE a 20 cm pie dish or cast-iron pan with the pastry.

SPOON the filling into the pie crust and bake for 45–50 minutes or until cooked through and golden.

REMOVE from the oven and allow to cool for 10 minutes before serving.

ENJOY warm or at room temperature.

NOTES AND INSPIRATION

Garnish the tart with a scattering of roasted pine nuts, sprouts or baby herbs. Drizzle the top with aged balsamic vinegar and serve with fresh tomato salad.

SPINACH AND RICOTTA CANNELLONI

I love making this simple and budget-friendly recipe when I'm entertaining. Any leftovers can easily be enjoyed cold straight out of the fridge or gently warmed and served with a side salad.

PROTEIN | VEGETARIAN | LOW GI | ENERGISING

INGREDIENTS

1 leek, sliced

2 tablespoons extra-virgin olive oil

400 g spinach or silverbeet (chard) blanched, squeezed and chopped (see Note)

400 g good-quality firm ricotta, strained

1 free-range egg

pinch of grated nutmeg

sea salt

800 g chopped, peeled tomatoes

2 garlic cloves, smashed

250 ml (1 cup) water

2 balls buffalo mozzarella, sliced

handful of fresh basil

2 quantities Spelt Crepes (p 246)

Serves 8

PREHEAT your oven to 180°C fan-forced.

SAUTÉ the leek with the olive oil on a low heat for 6 minutes until softened and combine with the spinach, ricotta, egg, nutmeg and a generous pinch of salt.

COMBINE tomatoes, garlic, pinch of salt and water in a saucepan and simmer for 15 minutes until reduced and slightly thickened.

SPREAD half of the tomato sauce over the base of an ovenproof baking dish.

LAY crepes on a flat working surface and top each with a few spoonfuls of ricotta spinach mixture. Roll up the crepes and arrange, seam side down in the baking dish, over the sauce. Pour the remaining sauce over the crepes and cover with mozzarella.

BAKE for 45 minutes and serve scattered with fresh basil.

NOTES AND INSPIRATION

You will require 400 g total weight of spinach once the water has been removed.

ROASTED VEGETABLE RATATOUILLE

This is my purely delicious roasted vegetable ratatouille that is filled with the nourishing flavours of summer. Leftovers can be enjoyed cold the next day as a salad or reheated and folded through al dente pasta.

GLUTEN-FREE | LOW CARB | PLANT-BASED | STRESS RELIEF

INGREDIENTS

4 zucchini, cut into thick slices

2 red onions, peeled and cut into thick wedges

3 red capsicums, cut into large chunks

6 Roma tomatoes, quartered

3 garlic cloves

2 tablespoons extra-virgin olive oil

generous pinch of sea salt

1–2 tablespoons good-quality aged balsamic vinegar or balsamic reduction

handful of chopped parsley

Serves 4

PREHEAT your oven to 180°C fan-forced.

COMBINE zucchini, onion, capsicum, tomatoes and garlic cloves in a baking dish and lightly coat with olive oil and a pinch of salt.

BAKE for 40–45 minutes or until vegetables have collapsed and look amazing and golden.

REMOVE from the oven and gently drizzle over balsamic and sprinkle with parsley.

SERVE at the table in the dish and enjoy.

NOTES AND INSPIRATION

Add 1 diced eggplant before roasting. Stir through al dente penne pasta or serve with grilled haloumi.

KALE AND ZUCCHINI FRITTATA

This is a delicious meal that I often make for my weekday lunches or dinners. It's high in antioxidants, minerals and protein to support a healthy metabolism.

VEGETARIAN | GLUTEN-FREE | PROTEIN | ANTIOXIDANT

INGREDIENTS

1 leek, finely sliced

2 tablespoons extra-virgin olive oil

1 bunch kale or cavolo nero, washed, trimmed and finely shredded

3 zucchini, cut into rounds

90 g baby spinach

6 free-range eggs

sea salt, to taste

90 g goat feta

Serves 6

PREHEAT your oven to 180°C fan-forced.

SAUTÉ leek in olive oil in an oven-proof frying pan until softened, then add the shredded kale and cook for 5 minutes until wilted. Add the zucchini and spinach and cook for a further 5 minutes.

BREAK eggs into a bowl, season with a little salt, then lightly whisk and pour over the vegetables in the pan.

CRUMBLE over the feta cheese and bake for 20–30 minutes until golden.

SERVE warm or at room temperature.

NOTES AND INSPIRATION

Serve with fresh leafy greens drizzled with lemon and olive oil.

ESSENTIALS + BASICS

FOOLPROOF PASTRY

Spelt flour adds a nutty flavour and boosts the nutritional profile of the pastry with more fibre, protein and minerals like magnesium and iron, while being gentler on digestion than regular wheat flour. When making this pastry, use your intuition and add a touch more water if needed to make into a dough.

WELLBEING | ALL NATURAL

INGREDIENTS

250 g (2 cups) spelt or plain flour

pinch of sea salt

170 g cold butter

60 ml (¼ cup) cold water

Makes enough for 1 pie or tart

COMBINE the flour and salt in a mixing bowl.

GRATE the butter into the flour.

LIGHTLY toss the butter through the flour. Using your fingertips, gently rub the butter into the flour until you have a sandy texture. Add the water and mix lightly with a knife until a soft dough is formed. Add a splash more water if needed.

FLATTEN the dough between 2 sheets of baking paper, then refrigerate for at least 30 minutes before using.

NOTES AND INSPIRATION

For a sweet dough, add 3 tablespoons of raw sugar or icing sugar to the flour before adding the water. Roll out the dough in oats instead of flour for a rustic oatmeal pastry.

SPELT ROUGH PUFF PASTRY

This rough puff pastry offers a wholesome twist on the classic, providing more fibre, protein and essential nutrients like magnesium and iron compared to store-bought versions. Wholemeal spelt supports better digestion, while the butter, when used in moderation, adds richness.

WELLBEING | ALL NATURAL | STRESS RELIEF

INGREDIENTS

250 g (2 cups) spelt flour

200 g cold butter

pinch of sea salt

125 ml (½ cup) iced water

Makes enough for 1 pie or tart

COMBINE the flour, butter and salt in a bowl and lightly mix with your hands, making sure the butter is evenly distributed.

POUR in the water and mix through with a knife until a rough dough forms. It's OK if it looks a bit messy. Shape and roll the dough using your hands into a rectangle about 35 cm long, dusting with flour as you go. Fold the short ends to meet in the centre and then fold the dough in half (book fold).

TURN the dough 90 degrees and roll out again, this time folding in 3 (letter fold). Repeat twice more, turning 90 degrees with a book fold then a letter fold, dusting with flour and working quickly.

WRAP in cling film and refrigerate for at least 1 hour. Roll the dough once more into a book fold, then a letter fold for a final layering. Rest and refrigerate for at least 1–2 hours before using.

ESSENTIALS + BASICS

GLUTEN-FREE PASTRY

This is the perfect pastry for all your gluten-free tarts and pies. The addition of eggs adds structure and stability to the dough, while butter adds flakiness and richness.

WELLBEING | HEART HEALTHY | ALL NATURAL

INGREDIENTS

250 g (2 cups) gluten-free flour, cup for cup

1 teaspoon gluten-free baking powder

pinch of sea salt

125 g cold butter, cut into cubes

2 large free-range eggs

Makes enough for 1 pie or tart

COMBINE the gluten-free flour, baking powder, salt and butter in a bowl. Using your fingers, rub the butter into the flour until the mixture is crumbly.

BEAT the eggs in a small bowl and mix through the flour to form a soft dough. Add 1 tablespoon of water if any flour or dry bits remain.

REST the dough in the fridge for 30 minutes to make it easier to roll.

USE in pies, tarts and anything you desire.

NOTES AND INSPIRATION

Add 3 tablespoons unrefined raw sugar or icing sugar for a sweeter pastry for fruit pies and tarts.

SIMPLE OLIVE OIL PASTRY

If you're on a low saturated fat, heart-healthy eating plan like my hubby Paul, then this is the perfect pastry. Easy to make and delicious to eat, it'll make you the superstar in the kitchen—and your body will thank you for it.

WELLBEING | HEART HEALTHY | ALL NATURAL

INGREDIENTS

250 g (2 cups) spelt flour

pinch of sea salt

1 teaspoon baking powder

80 ml (⅓ cup) extra-virgin olive oil

125 ml (½ cup) warm water

Makes enough for 1 pie or tart

COMBINE the spelt flour, salt and baking powder in a bowl.

POUR in the olive oil and warm water, then mix into a soft dough.

ROLL out immediately between 2 sheets of baking paper and use as required.

ENJOY as a base for savoury tarts and pies.

NOTES AND INSPIRATION

Add 2 tablespoons of sesame seeds when mixing the dough—it adds a lovely toasted aroma when baking. Alternatively, add a handful of rolled oats.

THE PERFECT CUSTARD

You can use whatever milk takes your fancy in this recipe; I love using full cream milk or if you're dairy-free, coconut milk works really well. I've given you a couple of different variations so that no matter what your eating style, you'll pretty much find the right custard to add the finishing touch to your favourite dessert.

PROTEIN | GLUTEN-FREE | WHOLEFOOD

INGREDIENTS

500 ml (2 cups) milk of any kind

2 teaspoons vanilla paste

2 free-range eggs

1 tablespoon arrowroot or kudzu

1 tablespoon honey or maple syrup

Makes 500 ml (2 cups)

HEAT milk and vanilla in a saucepan until almost boiled.

COMBINE eggs, arrowroot and honey in a stainless steel bowl and whisk well until creamy.

POUR hot milk over the eggs and whisk to combine.

TRANSFER the mixture back into the saucepan.

COOK over a very low heat, stirring constantly, until the mixture is thick and coats the back of a wooden spoon.

STRAIN custard into a clean bowl and cool quickly over iced water.

NOTES AND INSPIRATION

To make a vegan custard, heat 2 cups of almond or rice milk with 2 tablespoons maple syrup and 1 teaspoon vanilla extract until almost boiling. Thicken with a slurry made from 2 tablespoons arrowroot and a little water.

For no-cook custard, blend the pulp from 1 mango with ½ cup coconut milk and the juice of 1 orange. It's delicious served with passionfruit or fresh berries.

CASHEW CREAM WITH TAHITIAN VANILLA

I make my lush cashew cream on a weekly basis and love to spoon it over seasonal fruits, add it to smoothies or fold through my Bircher muesli. Cashews are high in the amino acid tryptophan, which helps to make serotonin—the hormone responsible for feelings of wellbeing. A hint of vanilla helps to elevate mood as well as reduce stress.

PROTEIN | RAW | SUPERFOOD | DAIRY-FREE

INGREDIENTS

1 cup raw cashews

180 ml (¾ cup) water

½ teaspoon Tahitian vanilla paste or powder

pinch of sea salt

Makes 500 ml (2 cups)

PLACE cashews in a bowl and cover completely with water. Soak for 2 hours and drain.

COMBINE cashews, water, vanilla and salt in a blender and blend for 30 seconds until smooth and creamy. If you like a thinner cream, you can add a touch more water.

POUR into a glass jar and store in the fridge until needed.

NOTES AND INSPIRATION

Add a pinch of ground cinnamon. Keeps for 5 days in the fridge.

VANILLA CRÈME PATISSIERE

This is my recipe for a classic thick custard, used to fill chocolate éclairs, tarts, vanilla slice, layer cakes, trifle or crumble or to simply enjoy straight from the pot. Made using whole eggs and cornflour to thicken, it's also gluten-free and not too sweet.

LOW GI | PROTEIN | GLUTEN-FREE

INGREDIENTS

375 ml (1½ cups) milk of your choice

2 free-range eggs

1 teaspoon vanilla extract

1 tablespoon raw honey

3 tablespoons gluten-free cornflour

Makes 500 ml (2 cups)

COMBINE all ingredients in a stainless-steel saucepan.

SIMMER, stirring over a medium heat, until the mixture starts to boil and thicken.

REMOVE from the stove and pour into a glass bowl. Strain through a fine sieve if you see any lumps.

COVER loosely to prevent a skin from forming.

COOL completely in the fridge.

DARK CHOCOLATE GANACHE

To make the perfect ganache, firstly, use the best-quality dark eating chocolate you can. Secondly, do not stir the chocolate through the cream until you've allowed it to sit for 3 minutes. This is crucial to make a smooth and silky ganache as the chocolate and cream unite in a perfect harmony. Thirdly, allow your ganache to cool gently at room temperature, not in the fridge, especially when using it to frost cakes or cupcakes.

STRESS RELIEF | ENERGISING | ALL NATURAL

INGREDIENTS

250 g good-quality 70% dark chocolate

250 ml (1 cup) cream

pinch of sea salt

Makes enough to ice 1 cake

CHOP the chocolate and place in a bowl.

HEAT the cream over a medium heat and remove just before boiling.

POUR the cream over the chocolate and add a pinch of salt.

LET sit for 3 minutes. Do not stir.

STIR gently after 3 minutes until smooth and glossy.

COOL at room temperature.

SPREAD over your favourite chocolate cake or cupcakes.

NOTES AND INSPIRATION

Any leftovers can be stirred through hot milk for an indulgent hot chocolate. Add another 60 g chocolate for a firm ganache that is lovely for chocolate truffles.

LUSH RICOTTA CRÈME

This decadent cream is a deliciously indulgent addition to any cake, tart or pie recipe. Perfect for éclairs, carrot cake or cupcakes.

PROTEIN | ALL NATURAL | GLUTEN-FREE

INGREDIENTS

500 g ricotta, firm, deli-style

1 tablespoon raw honey

1 teaspoon vanilla extract

½ teaspoon ground cinnamon

125 g mascarpone

Makes 625 ml (2½ cups)

COMBINE ricotta, honey, vanilla and cinnamon in a mixing bowl.

FOLD through mascarpone until well combined.

SPELT CREPES

I prefer eating crepes rather than pancakes and I use them for many sweet and savoury dishes. Try them in place of pasta in your next lasagne or enjoy for breakfast with blueberries and maple syrup.

ENERGISING | GUT FRIENDLY | ALL NATURAL

INGREDIENTS

3 large free-range eggs

250 ml (1 cup) milk

90 g (⅔ cup) spelt flour

pinch of sea salt

Serves 4

COMBINE ingredients in a bowl and whisk to form a smooth thin batter.

COOK wafer-thin crepes in a non-stick pan over a medium heat and set aside until required.

NOTES AND INSPIRATION

Top with yoghurt, honey and strawberries.

GLUTEN-FREE CREPES

Light and scrumptious, these delicate crepes will be the highlight of your weekend. Take your time and cook them in a good non-stick pan, then serve warm with a little honey and yoghurt.

ENERGISING | GUT FRIENDLY | ALL NATURAL

INGREDIENTS

5 free-range eggs

500 ml (2 cups) milk of your choice

150 g (1 cup) rice flour

3 tablespoons tapioca flour

pinch of sea salt

Serves 6

COMBINE all the ingredients in a bowl and whisk until smooth.

COOK wafer-thin crepes in a non-stick pan over a medium heat until all the batter is used.

NOTES AND INSPIRATION

For sweet crepes add 1 tablespoon unrefined raw sugar or honey. Top with ricotta and a drizzle of honey.

BLUEBERRY + CHIA JAM

Here is a quick, healthy blueberry jam recipe that won't spike your blood sugar and is perfect spread over freshly baked scones.

SUPERFOOD | OMEGA-3 | GLUTEN-FREE

INGREDIENTS

300 g fresh or frozen blueberries

1 teaspoon honey or a little stevia, to sweeten

juice of ½ lemon

1 teaspoon vanilla extract or paste

1½ tablespoons ground or whole chia seeds

Makes 500 ml (2 cups)

COMBINE blueberries, honey, lemon juice and vanilla in a saucepan.

SIMMER over a low heat for 5 minutes until the mixture looks syrupy.

ADD the chia seeds and mix through.

REMOVE from the heat and allow to stand for 5 minutes before pouring into a bowl and placing in the refrigerator.

REST for 1 hour until the jam forms a lovely gel-like consistency.

SPOON into a glass jar and use as required.

NOTES AND INSPIRATION

Replace chia with ½ cup of freshly made apple puree.

STRAWBERRY + VANILLA JAM

Make sure all your ingredients are at room temperature. This is really important for the emulsification process.

SUPERFOOD | OMEGA-3 | GLUTEN-FREE

INGREDIENTS

500 g strawberries, washed and hulled

1 teaspoon vanilla extract

2 fresh dates, pitted, or a little monk fruit sweetener

2 tablespoons white chia seeds

300 g raspberries

Makes 750 ml (3 cups)

COMBINE 250 g strawberries, vanilla, dates, chia and raspberries in a blender. Blend until smooth. Transfer to a bowl.

DICE the remaining strawberries and add them to the puree. Cover the bowl with cling film and refrigerate for at least 1 hour to allow the jam to thicken.

SPOON jam into glass jars and store in the refrigerator until needed. Keeps for 4 days.

NOTES AND INSPIRATION

Blend 2 tablespoons of this jam with homemade cashew or almond milk and a little ice for a healthy strawberry smoothie.

LABNEH

Labneh is a fresh cheese made from strained natural yoghurt. The acidophilus and lactobacilli cultures from yoghurt can nourish your immune system and support gut health. It's super easy to make yourself and the final texture and flavour tastes a little like Persian feta.

PROTEIN | ALL NATURAL | GUT FRIENDLY

INGREDIENTS

1 kg natural Greek yoghurt

Makes 500 g

LINE a sieve with a few layers of muslin or a nut milk bag and sit over a bowl ready to catch the whey.

SPOON in the yoghurt and cover the top with a piece of cling film.

PLACE another bowl or jar on top of the yoghurt to allow the extra whey to drain out.

REFRIGERATE for 24 hours, allowing the whey to strain.

STORE in a glass container in the fridge for up to 5 days or cover with olive oil, which will help it last for 2 weeks in the fridge.

NOTES AND INSPIRATION

Serve with sun-ripened heirloom tomatoes, fresh torn basil and cold-pressed olive oil or over salads, vegetables and poached eggs. Use labneh to make a yoghurt frosting to lavishly spread over cakes.

YOGHURT FROSTING

This is my signature yoghurt frosting I use on many of my healthy cakes and desserts. It's light on the palate and the tummy, and the taste is extraordinary.

ALL NATURAL | GUT FRIENDLY

INGREDIENTS

1 quantity Labneh (p 250)

60 ml (¼ cup) pure maple syrup

2 teaspoons vanilla extract

Makes enough to ice 1 cake

COMBINE labneh, maple syrup and vanilla in a bowl.

MIX well. Use to frost cakes and breads.

NOTES AND INSPIRATION

Use cream cheese, ricotta or quark if you don't have any labneh.

LIGHTENED UP CREAM CHEESE FROSTING

This low-sugar frosting delivers a creamy texture with added probiotics for gut health. It's more stable than yoghurt frosting and extremely versatile.

ALL NATURAL | GUT FRIENDLY

INGREDIENTS

250 g cream cheese, room temperature

120 ml (½ cup) thick Greek yogurt or labneh

2 tablespoons raw honey or pure maple syrup

zest of 1 lemon (optional)

Makes enough to ice 1 cake

COMBINE all the ingredients in a bowl until smooth and creamy.

LAVISHLY spread over cakes and cupcakes.

NOTES AND INSPIRATION

Play around and add other flavours to the frosting, such as matcha powder, cocoa powder or smashed raspberries.

INGREDIENTS I LOVE TO USE

ALMONDS One of my favourite nuts to use, whole almonds are incredibly delicious and are full of protein and vitamin E to help repair and nourish your body and immune system. The high fibre content supports digestive health, while the magnesium, calcium and potassium in almonds promote healthy nerve and muscle function. I love using Mandolé Orchard almond products, such as almond milk, as they always taste fresh, clean and delicious, which produce the best results.

ALMOND MEAL (GROUND ALMONDS) A popular gluten-free baking ingredient, almond meal is made from finely ground almonds and is loaded with protein, magnesium and potassium, which are essential for muscle and nerve function. Its vitamin E content can also help nourish the skin and promote a healthy immune system. Almond meal is also low carb, so it won't spike blood sugar.

AVOCADOS AND AVOCADO OIL Rich and creamy avocado oil is a wonderful source of monounsaturated fats that have healthy compounds to protect against inflammation and promote heart health. Avocados and their oil are rich with the antioxidant vitamin E, which helps support and protect the body against free radicals and promote a strong immune system as well as healthy skin and eyes. I love using avocados blended with cacao as a raw, nutrient-rich frosting for chocolate cake. I also love avocado oil in my chocolate cakes—it adds a wonderful buttery creaminess and flavour profile.

BROWN RICE FLOUR This flour is made from milling raw brown rice. It's high in protein and fibre to help keep blood sugars stable, and B vitamins for good brain and nerve function.

BUCKWHEAT FLOUR With its intense nutty flavour and grainy texture, buckwheat flour is one of my favourite flours to work with as it's incredibly versatile. It comes from a seed related to rhubarb and is low GI, high in amino acids and contains essential minerals such as manganese, magnesium, zinc and copper. The fibre in buckwheat is soluble, which can help to reduce blood cholesterol levels and promote regular bowel health.

BUTTER Good-quality butter is a rich source of essential fat-soluble vitamins A, E and K, antioxidants and trace minerals. It's best used at low to moderate cooking temperatures since the milk solids are prone to burning. Butter works beautifully in baking to add flavour and richness. I prefer to use Lurpak slightly salted butter in my recipes as it has a beautiful mild flavour and smooth texture, and it's made with no additives other than a touch of salt.

CASHEW NUTS Their velvet-like texture and subtle flavour make cashew nuts an amazing ingredient for dairy-free baking. They are rich in healthy fats and vitamin E, as well as a good source of minerals, particularly magnesium and zinc, which are essential for energy metabolism and nerve function. I love making homemade cashew nut milk scented with cinnamon and vanilla for a heavenly dairy-free milk to add in cakes, desserts and smoothies.

COCONUT SUGAR A deliciously toffee-like sweetener, coconut sugar is extracted sap from the blooms of the coconut and is coarser and darker than refined sugar. It has a low GI of 35 and contains potassium and phosphorous along with smaller amounts of magnesium, copper and zinc, making it preferable for steady blood-sugar levels.

DATES Incredibly caramel-like in texture and taste, fresh Medjool dates are absolutely delicious. They are a wonderful source of fibre, which is essential for maintaining a healthy digestive system, and contain notable amounts of vitamins B6 and B5, niacin, magnesium, manganese, copper and potassium—all important nutrients needed for healthy metabolism.

EXTRA-VIRGIN OLIVE OIL This oil is beautiful-tasting, velvety and teeming with health benefits: it's a rich source of antioxidants and monounsaturated fatty acids—one of the main reasons why the traditional Mediterranean diet is considered a smart move for heart health.

FRUIT Fresh and dried fruits are my top pick for sweeteners and are a wonderful way to naturally sweeten recipes with the added benefit of adding fibre and minerals. I love making my signature gluten-free banana bread or apple tea cake packed full of sun-ripened fruit, allowing the natural sugars from the fruit to sweeten the dish, rather than relying on added refined ingredients. There are no blood-sugar spikes and your body will thank you.

HONEY Raw, cold-extracted honey is antibacterial, antifungal and a powerful antioxidant, retaining most of its nutrients such as B group vitamins, vitamin C and smaller amounts of potassium and calcium. Unlike regular honey, raw honey retains enzymatic activity that may aid digestive function as it is not heat treated. I love the complexity and flavour that honey provides.

MACADAMIA NUTS Incredibly flavoursome and nourishing, macadamia nuts are high in anti-inflammatory, monounsaturated fats like olive oil and avocado, as well as iron and zinc. They make the most amazing base for the creamiest homemade nut butters!

MAPLE SYRUP This rich, golden syrup derived from the sap of the Canadian maple tree has a low GI, which means it doesn't give you that high blood-sugar spike that you can get with refined white sugar. Maple syrup is also considered low FODMAP and contains trace minerals like zinc, which is important for improving immunity, and manganese, which plays a crucial role in fat and carbohydrate metabolism.

MOLASSES Unlike refined sugar, molasses contains all the minerals and nutrients of the sugar cane plant. It's high in iron, manganese, potassium and copper, which all help support a healthy metabolism.

MONK FRUIT Monk fruit is a natural, zero-calorie sweetener derived from a small melon native to Southeast Asia. It contains compounds called mogrosides that provide intense sweetness—up to 200 times sweeter than sugar—without raising blood-sugar levels, making it ideal for people managing diabetes or following low-carb, ketogenic or anti-inflammatory diets. Unlike artificial sweeteners, monk fruit has no bitter aftertaste and is gentle on the digestive system. Its antioxidant properties and natural origin make it a popular choice for healthy baking, allowing you to enjoy sweetness without the guilt. It can be used across my recipes as an alternative to sugar.

OATS This wholesome grain is beautiful to bake with, imparting a crumbly texture to biscuits, cookies and muffins. Oats are also a good source of beta-glucan fibre that can help regulate your appetite and lower cholesterol. I love to use organically grown oats from Kialla Organics that are free from pesticides and chemicals. To make oat flour, just blitz rolled oats in a blender.

QUINOA An ancient superfood that is gluten-free and has a low GI of 53, quinoa is a complete protein, which means that it contains all the essential amino acids that the body needs for growth and repair. I normally bake with whole soaked or cooked quinoa rather than the flour, as it produces better results.

RAPADURA SUGAR Rapadura is pure sugar cane juice extracted from the sugar cane and then dehydrated. The result is a grainy sugar that retains its vitamins and minerals. The molasses has not been separated from the sugar, preserving the natural caramel taste of the sugar, and making it lovely in cakes and all sorts of baking.

RICE MALT SYRUP Rice malt syrup is a natural, fructose-free sweetener made from fermented brown rice, offering a mild, caramel-like flavour that blends beautifully into baked goods. It provides a steady release of energy thanks to its complex carbohydrates and low GI, making it a gentler alternative to refined sugar. Rice malt syrup is also suitable for those avoiding fructose and can enhance the texture and moisture of cakes, muffins and slices. Its smooth consistency makes it ideal for everything from healthy granola bars to guilt-free desserts, delivering sweetness without overwhelming the palate.

RYE FLOUR High in protein, B vitamins and magnesium, rye flour is also lower in gluten than regular wheat flour and a good source of fibre, helping to promote a healthy digestive system.

SPELT FLOUR Spelt is an ancient grain related to wheat and is lower in gluten than traditional wheat flours, making it great for people with wheat sensitivities. It's also high in protein and fibre with a low GI for sustained energy. I love to use fine-milled organic spelt flour from Kialla Organics, which is made without pesticides, as it's perfect for everyday baking. Spelt replaces traditional all-purpose flour cup for cup and the result is magnificent.

WALNUTS One of the more nutritionally superior nuts, walnuts are full of vitamin E, manganese, copper and omega-3 fatty acids. Walnuts have been linked to helping reduce the risk of heart disease and diabetes, while improving brain function and bone health.

CONVERSIONS + MEASUREMENTS

VOLUME OR LIQUID MEASURES

1 Australian teaspoon = 5 ml

1 Australian tablespoon = 20 ml

(North America, New Zealand and United Kingdom use 15 ml tablespoons)

CUP	METRIC	IMPERIAL
¼ cup	60 ml	2 fl oz
⅓ cup	80 ml	2¾ fl oz
½ cup	125 ml	4 fl oz
⅔ cup	160 ml	5½ flz oz
¾ cup	180 ml	6 fl oz
1 cup	250 ml	8¾ fl oz
2 cups	500 ml	17 fl oz
2½ cups	625 ml	21½ fl oz
4 cups	1 litre	35 fl oz

SPOON	METRIC
¼ teaspoon	1.25 ml
½ teaspoon	2.5 ml
1 teaspoon	5 ml
2 teaspoons	10 ml
1 tablespoon	20 ml

SOLID MEASURES

BUTTER

For baking I like to use grass-fed butter. One American stick of butter weighs 125 g (4 oz).

EGGS

I use organic free-range (60 g) eggs.

METRIC	IMPERIAL
30 g	1 oz
60 g	2 oz
125 g	4 oz
185 g	6 oz
250 g	8 oz
500 g	16 oz (1lb)
1 kg	35 oz (2 lb)

OVEN TEMPERATURES

OVEN BAKING

I use a fan-forced oven for all of my recipes.

CONVENTIONAL (NO FAN)	FAN-FORCED	FAHRENHEIT
140°C	120°C	250°F
150°C	130°C	270°F
160°C	140°C	280°F
170°C	150°C	300°F
180°C	160°C	320°F
190°C	170°C	325°F
200°C	180°C	360°F
220°C	200°C	400°F

LENGTH MEASURES

METRIC	IMPERIAL
3 cm	1 inch
5 cm	2 inches
10 cm	4 inches
15 cm	6 inches
20 cm	8 inches
25 cm	10 inches
30 cm	11 inches

CUP CONVERSIONS

(for ingredients commonly used in this book)

CUP	METRIC	IMPERIAL
1 cup almond meal (ground almonds)	100 g	3½ oz
1 cup wholemeal spelt flour	120 g	4 oz
1 cup rolled oats	100 g	3½ oz
1 cup desiccated coconut	100 g	3½ oz
1 cup cacao powder	120 g	4 oz
1 cup buckwheat flour	120 g	4 oz
1 cup rapadura/unrefined raw sugar	160 g	5½ oz
1 cup chia seeds	120 g	4 oz
1 cup brown rice flour	150 g	5¼ oz
1 cup rye flour	120 g	4 oz
1 cup raw cashew nuts	120 g	4 oz

INDEX

A

almonds 254
   pear and almond tart 144
Anzac biscuits, olive oil 193
apple
   apple and cinnamon bread 22
   apple and maple Dutch baby 25
   apple and maple tarte tatin 151
   apple and olive oil muffins with cream cheese frosting 162
   apple tea cake 84
   apple walnut cake 87
   carrot and apple muffins 165
   gluten-free apple crumble 131
   paleo apple cake 80
   wholesome apple pie 139
avocado 254
   avocado frosting 112
   avocado oil 254
   superfood chocolate tart 127

B

babka, Ciocia's 88
baked ricotta dumplings in tomato 212
banana
   banana and chia bread with espresso caramel 43
   banana, coffee and walnut bread 26
   banana oatmeal cookies 198
   blueberry and banana pancakes 21
   chocolate and banana bread 111
   French toast pudding with banana and blueberry 33
   gluten-free banana bread 29
beetroot
   red velvet cupcakes 108
berries
   baked blueberry oatmeal 17
   blueberry and banana pancakes 21
   blueberry and chia jam 249
   blueberry galette 140
   blueberry muffins 30
   chocolate raspberry muffins 177
   French toast pudding with banana and blueberry 33
   gluten-free blueberry scones 161
   peach and raspberry crumble 148
   rhubarb raspberry crumble 135
   rustic strawberry galette 147
   strawberry and vanilla jam 249
biscuits *see also* cookies
   Graham cracker biscuits 185
   olive oil Anzac biscuits 193
   vanilla tea biscuits 202
blueberries
   baked blueberry oatmeal 17
   blueberry and banana pancakes 21
   blueberry and chia jam 249
   blueberry galette 140
   blueberry muffins 30
   French toast pudding with banana and blueberry 33
   gluten-free blueberry scones 161
bread
   apple and cinnamon bread 22
   banana and chia bread with espresso caramel 43
   banana, coffee and walnut bread 26
   buttermilk loaf 47
   chocolate and banana bread 111
   fruit and rye loaf 34
   gluten-free banana bread 29
   gluten-free focaccia 52
   honey and ricotta bread 56
   keto pillow bread 59
   paleo pumpkin bread 39
   seeded rye, oat and sunflower bread 60
   seedy gluten-free bread 48
   spelt and kefir soda bread 55
   sweetcorn bread 63
   the perfect focaccia 51
breakfast baking
   apple and cinnamon bread 22
   apple and maple Dutch baby 25
   baked blueberry oatmeal 17
   banana, coffee and walnut bread 26
   blueberry and banana pancakes 21
   blueberry muffins 30
   cinnamon-dusted doughnuts 13
   French toast pudding with banana and blueberry 33
   fruit and rye loaf 34
   gluten-free banana bread 29
   Maui health crunch breakfast cookies 14
   quinoa pancakes with orange blossom honey 18
brown rice flour 254
brownie
   flourless chocolate brownie 120
   vegan chocolate sweet potato brownies 123
buckwheat
   buckwheat flour 254
   salted buckwheat cookies 189
   yoghurt buckwheat muffins 166
buns, potato 40
butter 254
buttermilk loaf 47

C

cakes *see also* cupcakes
   a beautiful lemon cake 100
   apple tea cake 84
   apple walnut cake 87
   best-ever fruit cake 75
   Ciocia's babka 88
   flourless orange cake 76

flourless salted chocolate
   cake 116
frosted hummingbird cake 79
garden olive oil cakes 99
garden zucchini cake 71
gluten-free chiffon cake 92
healthy carrot cake 72
naked chocolate cake 115
orange and olive oil tea cake 67
paleo apple cake 80
pumpkin fruit cake 91
semolina and olive oil syrup
   cake 68
the only chocolate cake you'll ever
   need 119
world's healthiest chocolate cake
   112
cannelloni, spinach and ricotta 228
caramel, espresso 44
carrot
   carrot and apple muffins 165
   healthy carrot cake 72
cashews 257
   cashew cream with Tahitian vanilla
      242
   lemon passionfruit cheesecake 83
cauliflower leek mac and cheese 211
cheese
   cauliflower leek mac and cheese
      211
cheesecake, lemon passionfruit 83
chia
   banana and chia bread with
      espresso caramel 43
   blueberry and chia jam 249
   strawberry and vanilla jam 249
chiffon cake, gluten-free 92
chocolate
   choc-chip olive oil cookies 201
   chocolate and banana bread 111
   chocolate raspberry muffins 177
   dark chocolate ganache 245
   flourless chocolate brownie 120
   flourless salted chocolate cake
      116
   healthy chocolate éclairs 107
   naked chocolate cake 115
   oatmeal choc-chip cookies 182
   OMG chocolate cupcakes 124
   salted buckwheat cookies 189
   superfood chocolate tart 127

the only chocolate cake you'll
   ever need 119
vegan choc-chip cookies 181
vegan chocolate sweet potato
   brownies 123
world's healthiest chocolate cake
   112
cinnamon
   apple and cinnamon bread 22
   cinnamon-dusted doughnuts 13
Ciocia's babka 88
coconut sugar 257
coffee
   banana, coffee and walnut bread
      26
   espresso caramel 44
cookies *see also* biscuits
   banana oatmeal cookies 198
   choc-chip olive oil cookies 201
   Maui health crunch breakfast
      cookies 14
   oatmeal choc-chip cookies 182
   peanut butter cookies 186
   raw Maui cookies 197
   salted buckwheat cookies 189
   tahini and hemp cookies 190
   vegan choc-chip cookies 181
corn
   sweetcorn bread 63
cream cheese frosting, lightened up
   253
crepes
   gluten-free crepes 246
   spelt crepes 246
crumble
   gluten-free apple crumble 131
   peach and raspberry crumble 148
   plum and hazelnut crumble 136
   rhubarb and custard, for 132
   rhubarb raspberry crumble 135
cupcakes
   gluten-free lamington cupcakes
      103
   lemon yoghurt cupcakes 96
   OMG chocolate cupcakes 124
   red velvet cupcakes 108
custard
   rhubarb and custard 132
   the perfect custard 241
   vanilla crème patissiere 242

D
dairy-free
   apple and cinnamon bread 22
   banana and chia bread with
      espresso caramel 43
   best-ever fruit cake 75
   cashew cream with Tahitian
      vanilla 242
   chocolate raspberry muffins 177
   espresso caramel 44
   gluten-free banana bread 29
   gluten-free blueberry scones 161
   lemon passionfruit cheesecake 83
   Maui health crunch breakfast
      cookies 14
   paleo pumpkin bread 39
   peanut butter cookies 186
   pumpkin scones 169
   raw Maui cookies 197
   world's healthiest chocolate cake
      112
dark chocolate ganache 245
dates 257
   espresso caramel 44
   lemon passionfruit cheesecake 83
   Maui health crunch breakfast
      cookies 14
   peach and raspberry crumble 148
   raw Maui cookies 197
   spelt and honey scones 174
   superfood chocolate tart 127
   vegan chocolate sweet potato
      brownies 123
doughnuts
   cinnamon-dusted doughnuts 13
dumplings
   baked ricotta dumplings in tomato
      212

E
éclairs, healthy chocolate 107
espresso caramel 44

F
feta
   kale, spinach and feta pie 207
   quinoa, spinach and feta muffins
      158
flourless chocolate brownie 120
flourless orange cake 76
flourless salted chocolate cake 116

focaccia
  gluten-free focaccia 52
  the perfect focaccia 51
foolproof pastry 237
French toast pudding with banana and blueberry 33
frittata, kale and zucchini 232
frosted hummingbird cake 79
frosting
  avocado frosting 112
  lightened up cream cheese frosting 253
  yoghurt frosting 253
fruit 257
  best-ever fruit cake 75
  fruit and rye loaf 34
  pumpkin fruit cake 91

G
galette
  blueberry galette 140
  roast pumpkin galette 224
  rustic strawberry galette 147
ganache, dark chocolate 245
garden zucchini cake 71
genius 15-minute pizza 219
gluten-free
  a beautiful lemon cake 100
  a better pavlova 95
  banana, coffee and walnut bread 26
  best-ever fruit cake 75
  blueberry and banana pancakes 21
  blueberry and chia jam 249
  blueberry muffins 30
  chocolate and banana bread 111
  chocolate raspberry muffins 177
  cinnamon-dusted doughnuts 13
  espresso caramel 44
  flourless chocolate brownie 120
  flourless orange cake 76
  flourless salted chocolate cake 116
  garden olive oil cakes 99
  gluten-free apple crumble 131
  gluten-free banana bread 29
  gluten-free blueberry scones 161
  gluten-free chiffon cake 92
  gluten-free crepes 246
  gluten-free focaccia 52
  gluten-free lamington cupcakes 103
  gluten-free pastry 238
  gluten-free scones 170
  healthy carrot cake 72
  honey and vanilla madeleines 194
  kale and zucchini frittata 232
  kale, spinach and feta pie 207
  keto pillow bread 59
  lemon passionfruit cheesecake 83
  lemon yoghurt cupcakes 96
  lush ricotta crème 245
  naked chocolate cake 115
  OMG chocolate cupcakes 124
  paleo apple cake 80
  paleo pumpkin bread 39
  peach and raspberry crumble 148
  pear and almond tart 144
  plum and hazelnut crumble 136
  potato buns 40
  quick and easy quiche 220
  quinoa pancakes with orange blossom honey 18
  quinoa, spinach and feta muffins 158
  red velvet cupcakes 108
  rhubarb and custard 132
  roasted vegetable ratatouille 231
  salted buckwheat cookies 189
  seedy gluten-free bread 48
  strawberry and vanilla jam 249
  sweetcorn bread 63
  tahini and hemp cookies 190
  the only chocolate cake you'll ever need 119
  the perfect custard 241
  vanilla crème patissiere 242
  vegan choc-chip cookies 181
  vegan chocolate sweet potato brownies 123
  vegetable lasagne 215
  world's healthiest chocolate cake 112
  yoghurt buckwheat muffins 166
Graham cracker biscuits 185

H
hazelnuts
  hazelnut crumble 136
  plum and hazelnut crumble 136
healthy carrot cake 72
healthy chocolate éclairs 107
hemp
  tahini and hemp cookies 190
honey 257
  honey and ricotta bread 56
  honey and vanilla madeleines 194
  orange blossom honey 18
  spelt and honey scones 174
hummingbird cake, frosted 79

J
jam
  blueberry and chia jam 249
  strawberry and vanilla jam 249

K
kale
  kale and zucchini frittata 232
  kale, spinach and feta pie 207
kefir
  spelt and kefir soda bread 55
keto pillow bread 59

L
labneh 250
lamington cupcakes, gluten-free 103
lasagne, vegetable 215
leek
  cauliflower leek mac and cheese 211
lemon
  a beautiful lemon cake 100
  lemon passionfruit cheesecake 83
  lemon yoghurt cupcakes 96
low GI
  apple and olive oil muffins with cream cheese frosting 162
  apple tea cake 84
  apple walnut cake 87
  baked blueberry oatmeal 17
  baked ricotta dumplings in tomato 212
  banana oatmeal cookies 198
  blueberry muffins 30
  Ciocia's babka 88
  cinnamon-dusted doughnuts 13
  flourless salted chocolate cake 116
  garden zucchini cake 71
  gluten-free scones 170

Graham cracker biscuits 185
healthy carrot cake 72
Maui health crunch breakfast cookies 14
oatmeal, pear and vanilla muffins 157
orange and olive oil tea cake 67
plum and hazelnut crumble 136
pumpkin fruit cake 91
red velvet cupcakes 108
seeded rye, oat and sunflower bread 60
spinach and ricotta cannelloni 228
spinach, ricotta and sweet potato tart 208
vanilla crème patissiere 242
world's healthiest chocolate cake 112
yoghurt buckwheat muffins 166
lush ricotta crème 245

M
mac and cheese, cauliflower leek 211
macadamias 257
madeleines, honey and vanilla 194
maple syrup 257
    apple and maple Dutch baby 25
    apple and maple tarte tatin 151
Maui health crunch breakfast cookies 14
molasses 257
monk fruit 258
muffins
    apple and olive oil muffins with cream cheese frosting 162
    blueberry muffins 30
    carrot and apple muffins 165
    chocolate raspberry muffins 177
    oatmeal, pear and vanilla muffins 157
    quinoa, spinach and feta muffins 158
    yoghurt buckwheat muffins 166

N
naked chocolate cake 115

O
oats 258

baked blueberry oatmeal 17
banana oatmeal cookies 198
Maui health crunch breakfast cookies 14
oatmeal choc-chip cookies 182
oatmeal, pear and vanilla muffins 157
olive oil Anzac biscuits 193
raw Maui cookies 197
seeded rye, oat and sunflower bread 60
olive oil
    apple and olive oil muffins with cream cheese frosting 162
    choc-chip olive oil cookies 201
    extra-virgin olive oil 257
    garden olive oil cakes 99
    olive oil Anzac biscuits 193
    orange and olive oil tea cake 67
    semolina and olive oil syrup cake 68
    simple olive oil pastry 238
orange
    caramelised oranges 76
    flourless orange cake 76
    orange and olive oil tea cake 67
    orange blossom honey 18
    orange syrup 68

P
paleo
    naked chocolate cake 115
    paleo apple cake 80
    paleo pumpkin bread 39
    peanut butter cookies 186
    raw Maui cookies 197
    the only chocolate cake you'll ever need 119
pancakes
    blueberry and banana pancakes 21
    quinoa pancakes with orange blossom honey 18
passionfruit
    lemon passionfruit cheesecake 83
pastry
    foolproof pastry 237
    gluten-free pastry 238
    simple olive oil pastry 238
    spelt rough puff pastry 237

pavlova
    a better pavlova 95
peach and raspberry crumble 148
peanut butter
    peanut butter cookies 186
    raw Maui cookies 197
pear
    oatmeal, pear and vanilla muffins 157
    pear and almond tart 144
    pears poached in wine 143
pies
    kale, spinach and feta pie 207
    wholesome apple pie 139
pizza, genius 15-minute 219
plum
    plum and hazelnut crumble 136
    rustic plum tart 152
potato buns 40
pumpkin
    paleo pumpkin bread 39
    pumpkin fruit cake 91
    pumpkin scones 169
    roast pumpkin galette 224

Q
quiche, quick and easy 220
quinoa 258
    quinoa pancakes with orange blossom honey 18
    quinoa, spinach and feta muffins 158

R
rapadura sugar 258
raspberries
    chocolate raspberry muffins 177
    peach and raspberry crumble 148
    rhubarb raspberry crumble 135
ratatouille, roasted vegetable 231
raw Maui cookies 197
red velvet cupcakes 108
rhubarb
    rhubarb and custard 132
    rhubarb raspberry crumble 135
rice malt syrup 258
ricotta
    baked ricotta dumplings in tomato 212
    honey and ricotta bread 56
    lush ricotta crème 245

ricotta *continued*
- spinach and ricotta cannelloni 228
- spinach, ricotta and sweet potato tart 208
- zucchini and ricotta tart 223

roasted vegetable ratatouille 231
rustic strawberry galette 147
rye
- fruit and rye loaf 34
- rye flour 258
- seeded rye, oat and sunflower bread 60

S

scones
- gluten-free blueberry scones 161
- gluten-free scones 170
- pumpkin scones 169
- spelt and honey scones 174
- ugly scones 173

seeds
- seeded rye, oat and sunflower bread 60
- seedy gluten-free bread 48

semolina and olive oil syrup cake 68
spelt 258
- garden zucchini cake 71
- honey and ricotta bread 56
- orange and olive oil tea cake 67
- spelt and honey scones 174
- spelt and kefir soda bread 55
- spelt crepes 246
- spelt rough puff pastry 237

spinach
- kale, spinach and feta pie 207
- quinoa, spinach and feta muffins 158
- spinach and ricotta cannelloni 228
- spinach, ricotta and sweet potato tart 208
- vegan spinach tart with tofu ricotta 227

strawberries
- rustic strawberry galette 147
- strawberry and vanilla jam 249

sweet potato
- spinach, ricotta and sweet potato tart 208
- vegan chocolate sweet potato brownies 123

sweetcorn bread 63

T

tahini and hemp cookies 190
tarte tatin, apple and maple 151
tarts
- apple and maple tarte tatin 151
- pear and almond tart 144
- rustic plum tart 152
- spinach, ricotta and sweet potato tart 208
- superfood chocolate tart 127
- vegan spinach tart with tofu ricotta 227
- zucchini and ricotta tart 223

tomato
- baked ricotta dumplings in tomato 212
- smashed tomato sauce 215

U

ugly scones 173

V

vanilla
- cashew cream with Tahitian vanilla 242
- honey and vanilla madeleines 194
- oatmeal, pear and vanilla muffins 157
- strawberry and vanilla jam 249
- vanilla crème patissiere 242
- vanilla tea biscuits 202

vegan
- banana and chia bread with espresso caramel 43
- pumpkin scones 169
- superfood chocolate tart 127
- vegan choc-chip cookies 181
- vegan chocolate sweet potato brownies 123
- vegan spinach tart with tofu ricotta 227

vegetable lasagne 215
vegetable ratatouille, roasted 231

W

walnuts 258
- apple walnut cake 87
- banana, coffee and walnut bread 26

wholesome apple pie 139
world's healthiest chocolate cake 112

Y

yoghurt
- labneh 250
- lemon yoghurt cupcakes 96
- yoghurt buckwheat muffins 166
- yoghurt cream 166
- yoghurt frosting 253

Z

zucchini
- garden zucchini cake 71
- kale and zucchini frittata 232
- zucchini and ricotta tart 223

THANK YOU

What a joy it has been to bring *Feel Good Baking* to life! A celebration of goodness, love and the simple magic that happens when you bake from the heart.

To my husband, Paul, my partner in life, love, and all things beautiful. For over thirty-five years, you've stood beside me, camera in hand and heart wide open. Your photographs dance across these pages like sunlight on a warm cake. Thank you for your calm presence, your refined taste buds, and for always believing in the dream. You make everything better.

To the endlessly talented Vanessa Russell, your design has sprinkled this book with elegance and soul. You've taken my vision and wrapped it in beauty. Working with you is always a joy and a creative adventure I cherish.

To Ben Ball and the fabulous team at Simon & Schuster, thank you for your perseverance, persistence and for bringing this book to life with such care and sparkle. I'm so grateful for your support.

To Natalie and the wonderful crew at Elixinol Wellness, thank you for embracing my journey and The Healthy Chef with such generous hearts. Your belief means the world to me.

And to every beautiful soul who has supported me, those who've baked my recipes, shared their stories, or simply sent a kind word my way, thank you.

Here's to warm ovens, good company, and the happiness that rises when we bake with love.

With all my heart,
Teresa

ABOUT TERESA

Known around the world as The Healthy Chef, Teresa Cutter is recognised as a pioneer in the field of wellness and healthy cooking, and lives by the motto 'keep it simple and make it yourself'.

Teresa's recipes focus on Mediterranean-style recipes that are simple, easy, healthy and delicious. Drawing on a unique blend of skills as a classically trained chef, nutritionist and accredited fitness trainer, Teresa shares her recipes via her social media, TV appearances, cooking masterclasses and magazine articles.

Teresa's recipes have been featured in *TIME* magazine in the US, *The Sydney Morning Herald*, *The Daily Telegraph* and *Delicious* magazine. Teresa has also appeared on numerous TV shows, including *Today*, *Sunrise*, *The Morning Show* and *The Biggest Loser Australia*.

Teresa is the author of ten health and wellness cookbooks including *Earth to Table*, *Purely Delicious*, *Simple Healthy Recipes* and *The 80/20 Diet*, focusing on nutrient-rich recipes for optimal health, reaching a wide global audience and setting new trends in health-focused cuisine.

She has also won numerous awards, including a gold medal at the Salon Culinaire, an international cooking competition for chefs. She also came second in Australia in the NABBA Fitness Figure Championships and won a silver medal for road cycling at the Southwest Games in Western Australia. Teresa's hobbies include Pilates, cycling and painting.